AMONG THE MYSTICS

AMONG THE MYSTICS

BY

WILLIAM FAIRWEATHER
M.A., D.D.(Edin.)

EDINBURGH
T. & T. CLARK, 38 GEORGE STREET
1936

TO
MY WIFE

BV
5075
F3

PRINTED IN GREAT BRITAIN BY
MORRISON AND GIBB LIMITED
FOR
T. & T. CLARK, EDINBURGH

PREFACE

MORE must not be expected from this book than is suggested by the title. It does not claim to be a complete treatment of Mysticism, either historical, philosophical, expository, or critical. While none of these aspects of it has been ignored, the main object has been to set down the results of some studies relating to a subject which, in spite of the increasing attention being devoted to it in the present century,[1] particularly since the Great War, cannot yet be said to have come to its own in our theological literature.

I have had chiefly in view that section of the public which may presumably desire something more detailed than, for example, E. C. Gregory's *Introduction*, and less scientifically thorough than W. R. Inge's excellent *Bampton Lectures*. That older work which for half a century had the field practically to itself—R. A. Vaughan's *Hours with the Mystics*—though racily written, and containing much that is serviceable, is marred by the almost flippant form of its conception, and by its too contemptuous attitude towards the Roman Church. The works of Baron von Hügel, and also with certain qualifications those of Miss E. Underhill, merit cordial recognition, and more attention than I have been able to give to them. As it is, with an acknowledgement of indebtedness to the article "Mysticism" by Professor A. Seth (Pringle Pattison) in the *Encyclopædia Britannica*, to the Gifford Lectures by Professor William James on *The Varieties of Religious Experience*, to Dr. Alexander Whyte's appreciations of

[1] See the interesting bibliography appended to Mrs. E. Herman's fine book, *The Meaning and Value of Mysticism*. This work is distinctive in respect of the emphasis which it lays upon Mysticism "as an active factor in the life and thought of to-day."

William Law and *Jacob Behmen*, to the treatise by
E. Herman already mentioned, and especially to Dr. Inge's
valuable work on *Christian Mysticism*, this little book is
issued for what it is worth, and in the hope that other and
abler pens may contribute towards the further elucidation
of a hitherto noticeably neglected theme.

In dealing with post-Reformation Mysticism, which
was much more Catholic than Protestant, I have deemed
it advisable to illustrate it by brief biographical sketches
of some of its prominent representatives, together with
selections from their writings, rather than to enter upon
any general discussion of their doctrinal tenets. For this
the reason is obvious ; apart from their increased emphasis
on Quietism, they added little or nothing to the conclusions, either philosophical or theological, arrived at
by their predecessors.

The following pages, it may be added, are written
from the point of view that Mysticism is not, as Miss
Underhill maintains, confined to Christianity,[1] but is a
feature in other religions as well. This, of course, is not
to deny that there is a specifically Christian Mysticism ;
still less is it to admit that such Mysticism is limited to
the Roman Catholic Church, as Harnack and Herrmann
assert.

That a wider knowledge of Mysticism is a desideratum
of the present day can scarcely be questioned. Probably
the very name has a deterrent effect upon many minds,
seeing it has come to be too much associated with dreamy
visionaries without aptitude for the ordinary affairs of
life. In reality history tells another tale. As William
James has said : " Saint Ignatius was a mystic, but his
mysticism made him assuredly one of the most powerful,
practical, human machines that ever lived." In many
other instances, too, mystics have shewn first-rate
business talent. Yet this is not their *métier*. The main
concern of the mystic is avowedly prayer and contemplation.

---

[1] See especially *The Mystic Way*, in the preface to which she says :
" I believe that the emergence of Mysticism as a definite type of
spiritual life coincides with the emergence of Christianity itself in
the person of its Founder." She denies that it has any of its
roots in Philo or in Neoplatonism.

As the attitude of Dr. Keate, whom George III. appointed headmaster of Eton in 1809, and of whom André Maurois says that " he feared Mysticism more than indifference," still persists, it should not be forgotten that there are mystics *and* mystics, and that the fantastic vagaries of some do not warrant indiscriminate censure of all. If the keen hostility of Ritschl and his school in Germany has not spread to our own country, it has presumably helped to produce the impression that Mysticism is matter only for neglect or animadversion. It is significant that a distinguished and highly esteemed theologian of our day, while rightly protesting against the isolation of the glorified Redeemer from the historic Jesus, should have been content to speak in no measured terms of " an unbridled and capricious mysticism," " a type of sentiment and belief totally dissimilar from the religion of the New Testament," [1] without a qualifying word. Is this quite fair ? No one expects that the mystics should be exempt from reasonable and just criticism, but surely their good points are also worthy of recognition. Their deep spirituality, self-surrender, and yearning after close communion with God, are beyond dispute, and stand in marked contrast to the materialism of our own age, to which the perusal of their idealistic writings might well prove a salutary antidote. And since, above all, they have served in a marked degree to awaken and preserve spiritual life within the Christian Church, their religious significance cannot without loss be ignored. Are we not more likely to reach a true evaluation of " Mystical Theology " by duly weighing its merits and demerits than by resorting to the short and easy method of wholesale ostracism ? In relation to this whole question the position of Professor Haering, a German Protestant, seems the most tenable. This writer draws a clear distinction between the genuine type of mysticism and those aspects of it which reject a historical revelation in the interests of a chimerical and visionary theosophy. Only through this line of approach can Mysticism ever come to its rights—a consummation devoutly to be wished, especially if Professor Bernhard Duhm is right in saying that " religion is a mystical thing

[1] H. R. Mackintosh, *The Person of Jesus Christ*, p. 378.

from beginning to end." Meanwhile it can at all events
positively be claimed that any Christian soul may find
edification in the writings of Catholic mystics like St.
Teresa and St. Francis de Sales, or in those of a Protestant
mystic like William Law.

W. FAIRWEATHER.

Edinburgh, 1936.

" He (Novalis) much loved, and had assiduously studied Jacob Böhme and other mystical writers; and was, openly enough, in good part a mystic himself. Not indeed what we English, in common speech, call a Mystic; which means only a man whom we do not understand, and, in self-defence, reckon or would fain reckon a Dunce. Novalis was a Mystic, or had an affinity with Mysticism, in the primary and true meaning of that word, exemplified in some shape among our own Puritan Divines. . . . In this sense great honours are recorded of Mysticism : Tasso, as may be seen in several of his prose writings, was professedly a Mystic ; Dante is regarded as a chief man of that class. Nevertheless, with all due tolerance or reverence for Novalis's Mysticism, the question still returns on us : How shall we understand it, and in any measure shadow it forth ? How may that spiritual condition, which by its own account is like pure Light, be represented by mere Logic-Painters, mere Engravers, we might say, who, except copper and burin, producing the most finite black-on-white, have no means of representing anything ? . . . ' What is Mysticism ? ' asks Novalis. ' What is it that should come to be treated mystically ? Religion, Love, Nature, Polity. All select things *(alles Auserwählte)* have a reference to Mysticism. . . .' Let there be free scope for Mysticism, or whatever else honestly opposes it. A fair field and no favour, and the right *will* prosper ! . . . Mysticism, whatever it may be, should, like other actually existing things, be understood in well-informed minds. We have observed, indeed, that the old-established laugh on this subject has been getting rather hollow of late ; and seems as if ere long it would in a great measure die away."

THOMAS CARLYLE.

CONTENTS

PART III

POST-REFORMATION CHRISTIAN MYSTICISM

A. *CATHOLIC*

1. SPANISH MYSTICS

(1) *Santa Teresa* (1515–82)

(2) *St. Juan of the Cross* (1542–91)

(3) *Miguel Molinos* (1627–96)

2. French Mystics

(1) *François de Sales* (1567–1622) [*and Madame de Chantal*]

(2) *Madame Guyon* (1648–1717) [*and Fénelon*]

B. *PROTESTANT*

1. GERMAN MYSTICS

Jacob Boehme as Chief Representative

2. ENGLISH MYSTICS

(1) *The Cambridge Platonists*

(2) *William Law* (1686–1761)

PART IV

THE BASIC PRINCIPLES AND MAIN FEATURES OF CHRISTIAN MYSTICISM

I. BASIC PRINCIPLES

II. DISTINCTIVE FEATURES

PART V

MYSTICISM IN ENGLISH POETRY

William Wordsworth (1770–1850) *as Leading Representative*

AMONG THE MYSTICS

INTRODUCTORY

WHAT is meant by Mysticism ? To this the answer
is not easy. Many definitions of the term have
been attempted, but none can be called quite satisfactory.
According to R. A. Vaughan, " Mysticism, whether in
religion or philosophy, is that form of error which mistakes
for a Divine manifestation the operations of a merely
human faculty "—a very defective, not to say biased and
erroneous description. Dr. Inge defines it as " the attempt
to realize, in thought and feeling, the immanence of the
temporal in the eternal, and the eternal in the temporal."
" Mysticism," says Pfleiderer, " is the immediate feeling of
the unity of self with God ; it is nothing, therefore, but the
fundamental feeling of religion, the religious life at its very
heart and centre." Closely akin to this is the language of
Edward Caird : " It is religion in its most concentrated
form ; it is that attitude of the mind in which all other
relations are swallowed up in the relation of the soul to
God." Although abstract, this statement is essentially
true, and perhaps no better general description can be
given. As a " rough statement," and recognizing that it
leaves unsolved many questions arising out of it, Mrs. E.
Herman characterizes Mysticism as " a direct inward
apprehension of the Divine." In the words of Professor
A. Seth (Pringle-Pattison), " It appears in connexion with
the endeavour of the human mind to grasp the Divine
Essence or the ultimate reality of things, and to enjoy the
blessedness of actual communion with the highest. The
first is the philosophic side of Mysticism ; the second, its
religious side." In the one aspect it is distinguished from
ordinary pantheism by its religious impulse to reach
ineffable union with the Divine. Hence the mystic's

I

tendency to subordinate everything to the contemplative
life, and to concern himself only with the relation between
himself and God. The identity with God to which he
aspires cannot be reached through any progressive advance
in knowledge, but by direct intuition only. In its practical
aspect Mysticism stands for direct fellowship with God
apart from all external media, not excepting Scripture
itself—a fellowship attainable only through an ecstatic
union tantamount to a participation in the Divine nature.
Thus " God ceases to be an object, and becomes an
experience." It is the view of the Ritschlian school that
Mysticism is a delusion, and that true Christianity is nothing
but faith in the Christ of history. Harnack says " Mysticism is rationalism applied to a sphere above reason," and
both he and Hermann regard it as merely a special feature
of Roman Catholicism.

The resultant impression conveyed by a variety of
efforts [1] to state the distinctive qualities of Mysticism
suggests that, like life itself, it can perhaps never be really
defined. Nor is it correctly viewed as a term specially
applicable to any particular religious cult. While, however,
the vague meaning attaching to the word constitutes a
preliminary difficulty in any discussion of the subject, it
may safely be said that it usually connotes a peculiar
illumination of the soul, and a direct contemplation of the
Divine, not shared by the generality of religious professors.
Mysticism sets less store by objective written revelation
than by the inner perception of the mind, and projects the
creation of its own dreams beyond the pale of experience.
In its visionary enthusiasm it is apt frequently to mistake
its own shadows for realities.[2] There is no doubt a mystical
factor in every religion properly so called. It occurs in the
Indian Vedas, in the Hebrew Psalms, in the Greek Platonism, in the Pauline Epistles, and also, it may be added, in
the Hegelian Philosophy, and in English Poetry. That it
has a legitimate place in the sphere of religion will scarcely
be disputed, yet it is equally indisputable that in what
is known as Mysticism generally there is an extreme and
disproportionate development of this factor. The con-

---

[1] For further examples, see Inge, *Christian Mysticism*, Appendix A.
[2] See the reference to " an unbridled and capricious mysticism,"
by H. R. Mackintosh, *op. cit.* p. 378 f.

sciousness of self is lost in the exclusive consciousness of God, whereas in religion there is necessarily involved an equal reaction of these two elements. By its emphasis upon the one and its indifference to the other the true balance is destroyed. The result is that in his ambition to attain union with the Divine the mystic is liable to be either landed in wild pantheistic speculation or led into the practice of extreme bodily austerities and the cultivation of nebulous ecstatic raptures. Not that " mystics can see anything in a fog, just anything, if it's only thick enough," [1] but broadly speaking it may not unfairly be said that in any of its aspects—ascetic, quietistic, visionary, or ecstatic —mysticism implies either a forced restraint or an un-natural excitement of the human faculties and feelings dis-tasteful to the bulk of mankind. Nor has it escaped serious injury through the failure of some of its supporters to dis-criminate between its essential features and its perceptible extravagances. On the whole, however, it is true to say that the mystic is " the real scientist of the spirit."

In view of the frequent depreciatory use of the term " mystical " to designate any vague or sentimental opinion, it seems advisable to restrict its religious significance to certain characteristic features. On this principle Professor William James suggests four marks by which mystical states of consciousness may justly be distinguished. These are (1) Ineffability. They defy expression, and can neither be impartial nor described. (2) Noetic quality. They are states of knowledge, illumination, and revelation. (3) Transiency. After an hour or two at most they fade away. (4) Passivity. The mystic's own will is in abeyance.

To the question, " Can we invoke the mystic range of consciousness as authoritative ? " Dr James replies as follows : " (1) Mystical states, when well developed, usually are, and have the right to be, absolutely authori-tative over the individuals to whom they come. (2) No authority emanates from them which should make it a duty for those who stand outside of them to accept their revela-tions uncritically. (3) They break down the authority of the non-mystical or rationalistic consciousness, based upon the understanding and the senses alone. They shew it to be only one kind of consciousness. They open out

[1] H. M. Tomlinson, *Gallion's Reach*, p. 228.

the possibility of other orders of truth, in which, so far as anything in us vitally responds to them, we may freely continue to have faith." [1]

This limitation of the use of the term "mystical" as applied to religion certainly supplies a wholesome corrective to the vaguely indiscriminate usage which had hitherto been too much in vogue.

[1] *The Varieties of Religious Experience*, pp. 380 ff., 422 ff.

PART I

THE RISE OF MYSTICISM IN THE EAST

HISTORICALLY, Mysticism is usually attributed to a revolt against scholastic intellectualism. It is a protest against hard and stiff dogmatic pronouncements in the affairs of the soul. From bondage to a religion of authority, it seeks to escape by breathing the fresh air of a religion of the spirit. " Thus Brahmanism called forth Buddhism ; the Talmud, the Kabbala ; the Mohammedan Korán-worship, Súfism ; and, within the pale of Christendom, the Spanish Inquisition called forth the Alombrados, Jesuitism, Quietism, Jansenism, etc." [1] The separate phenomena are all connected, however, by a real affinity.

At the outset it may be advisable to consider the extent to which Mysticism is reflected in the Scriptures.

The trend of Jewish religion was not towards mysticism. Rather did it emphasize the individuality of both God and man. While acutely conscious of the insignificance of man in contrast to the majesty and power of God, it never lost a sense of the reality of the visible world, or of the responsibilities entailed in the routine of daily existence. So far from sharing the Platonic obsession of an ideally perfect world existing " beyond," it stressed the duty of man here and now, in the actual circumstances of everyday life, to respond to the demands of the moral law, and to make this manifest by the careful performance of outward religious observances. Its point of view is that it is for God to speak, and for man to listen ; for God to command, and for man to obey. Thus the Jew's realistic conception of the visible creation was conditioned by a firm faith in the sovereign rule of Omnipotence. While not inherently mystical, Judaism did, however, share the mystic's thirst for God as frequently expressed in the Psalms, though mostly in strict combination with a reverential regard for

[1] J. P. Lange, article " Mysticism " in *Schaff-Herzog Encyc.*

law and a keen appreciation of the external aspect of piety.[1] Conformably to this attitude of the righteous will be his recompense (Is 33[17]). Although in the OT expression is given to the thought of the chosen people as " married " to their Maker (Is 54[15]; Jer 3[14]), there is no reason to suppose that the later mystical view of the Song of Solomon, so long and so unwarrantably prevailing in the Christian Church, was based upon any Jewish interpretation of that love song.

The mystical element in the NT calls for more consideration. In the Synoptic Gospels, written mainly from the objective standpoint of historical narrative, there is naturally not much to our purpose beyond a few stray sayings embodying what may be called the essence of mysticism. To the pure in heart is promised the vision of God (Mt 5[8]), and the assurance is given that " the kingdom of God is within (or among) you " (Lk 17[21]). In the declaration: " Inasmuch as ye have done it unto one of the least of these my brethren, ye have done it unto me " (Mt 25[40]), the oneness of Jesus with His disciples is clearly taught. And the great principle of gain through sacrifice is definitely set forth: " Whosoever will save his life (=soul) shall lose it; but whosoever will lose his life (=soul) for my sake, the same shall save it " (Lk 29[24]).

When we pass to the Fourth Gospel we are in a distinctly mystical atmosphere. To realize its Christian ideal is the persistent aim of the mystic. In seeking direct fellowship with God he takes as his model the personal practice of Jesus, who through prayer kept in constant touch with His Father. Behind all His activities and teaching lay the fact of personal communion with God. The consciousness of Sonship was begotten of this spiritual love experience, which, although unique (Mt 11[22]), the Christian mystic strives to share to the point of union with Deity (Jn 17[20ff.]). Though pre-eminently the mystic among " the Twelve," St. John's main purpose was to interpret theologically the supreme significance of the Incarnation. He lays great emphasis upon the Person of the Word or Logos of God, and upon the historical fact that He " was made flesh and tabernacled among us " as the Revealer of God and Giver of eternal life. In his First Epistle the confession that

[1] Pss 42[1-2], 63[1-2], 73[25f.], 119[10. 97. 174].

Jesus Christ is come in the flesh he posits as the test of the possession of the spirit of truth, and the withholding of this confession as evidence of the spirit of error (4³ᶠ·⁶). For him there is no spiritual revelation of God apart from its material and historical counterpart. His conception of Christianity is based less upon the Cross than upon the Incarnation. As the Son came in order to reveal the Father, so it is the office of the Holy Spirit to reveal the Son, and to lead Christian disciples into an ever fuller understanding of His doctrine (Jn 16¹²).

Pervading St. John's writings there is a decidedly Platonic strain, traceable perhaps to the Jewish-Alexandrian philosophy of Philo (but see below). He differentiates between the true or real world of light which is " above," and " this world " which is the realm of darkness and evil. The Incarnation discloses in this world the essential nature of the world above, the world of spirit and life (1 Jn 2⁸). Only through faith in Christ's mediation can we attain to the knowledge of God. In Him was life, and the life which was eternally in Him is the unfailing light of men (Jn 1⁴). To this the writer bears emphatic testimony from his own experience : " For of his fulness have we received " (Jn 1¹⁶). Salvation implies communion and union with Christ (15⁴) and with God (17²⁰ᶠᶠ·). In an age when many shewed impatience at the delay of the Parousia, St. John pointed out that the Christian salvation is not merely a thing of the future, but can be experienced in reality here and now. Even the judgement is not postponed to the last day, for " he that believeth not hath been judged already " (Jn 3¹⁸). This does not mean, however, that there will be no future judgement. On this subject he represents our Lord as adopting the traditional standpoint, and, while investing the doctrine of salvation with a special aspect of his own, does so without deviating from the primitive Christian eschatology. Finally, in the Johannine conception of salvation marked emphasis is laid on its ethical character, " Whosoever doeth not righteousness is not of God " (1 Jn 3¹⁰). Thus also fellowship with God and with one another is symbolically described as walking in the light (1⁶ᶠ·), and as abiding in Christ's love and bearing fruit as branches in the true vine (Jn 15¹⁻¹⁶). The direct religious significance of union with Christ is emblematically set forth

under the idea of eating and drinking the flesh and blood of
Christ (Jn 6[53ff.])—words akin to the designation of Him as
the bread of life (6[35]). Besides the personal union between
the individual soul and Christ there is also a mystical union
between Him and the Church and between its members
(17[21]). To those who enjoy such a fellowship there comes
an absolute conviction of their spiritual well-being that
needs no support from external evidences. So much value
does the writer attach to this that he ascribes it to the
indwelling of the Holy Ghost, the Comforter (16[7, 13]).
This spiritual illumination and unification is not, however,
a fixed quantity bestowed once for all, but a gradual and
progressive approach toward union with Him in whom
dwells the glory given Him by the Father and reserved for
those given Him out of the world (17[22]).

Mysticism is even more characteristic of the Pauline
than of the Johannine theology. Personal experience of
the Divine presence vibrates like a strong chord through
St. Paul's Epistles. He tells how God " revealed His
Son " in him (Gal 1[12f.]). " I am crucified with Christ," he
says, " yet not I, but Christ liveth in me " (2[20]). And
again, " God hath sent forth the Spirit of his Son into our
hearts, crying, ' Abba, Father ' " (4[6]). It is his prayer
" that Christ may dwell in your hearts by faith," and " that
ye might be filled with all the fulness of God " (Eph 3[17-19]).
Further, " God . . . hath shined in our hearts, to give the
light of the knowledge of the glory of God in the face of
Jesus Christ " (2 Co 4[6]). In the latter epistle is also used
the striking figure of the mirror : " We all, with unveiled
face reflecting as a mirror the glory of the Lord, are transformed into the same image from glory to glory " (3[18]).
These and other passages testify to the apostle's consciousness of the Divine presence as bound up with the human
spirit in the case of believing men. His Christianity is
based, not upon man's teaching, nor upon external evidences, but upon the fact that Christ had " appeared "
to him (Ac 26[16]). His claim is that while the carnal mind
is incapable of discerning the " mystery " or " hidden
wisdom of God," this is " revealed " to the receptive soul
by His Spirit (Eph 3[9] ; cf. Col 1[29]). In his rebound from
the law he declares that " where the Spirit of the Lord is
there is liberty " (2 Co 3[17]), and boldly refers moral questions

to the arbitrament of the inner life as expressing the mind of Christ (1 Co 3$^{15f.}$). His ethic is based upon his experience of the indwelling Spirit (Ro 8^9) by whose coming man is renewed and raised to a new life (Eph 4$^{23f.}$).

In the Pauline Epistles there are manifest traces of the influence of the Stoic philosophy, and of acquaintance with the language of the Mystery Religions which had gained many adherents throughout the Roman empire before his day; but it is clear that the main element in his conviction of a Divine and encompassing presence is what had actually been experienced by himself personally, as well as by companies of those to whom he had carried the gospel. " To me to live is Christ," he says (Ph 1^{21}), and this sums up all. The Christian becomes a new creature in Christ Jesus (2 Co 5^{17}), sharing with other believers in His experiences of suffering and of joy, living over again the Christ-life, overcoming evil with good (Ro 12^{21}), and ultimately partaking in His glory (Ro 8^{17}).

Paul's experience of ecstasy (2 Co 12) represents him as having been involuntarily " caught up into the third heaven," where he heard things to which a man's voice could not give utterance. They were disclosed to him solely for his own enlightenment. Of his further transportation to the upper paradise of God he says that in his normal condition he will make no boast. The mode in which the vision took place is undefined, but he leaves it to be understood that it was no ordinary ecstatic trance, and that it cannot therefore be reckoned as a real example of mysticism. Moreover, while the Pauline Epistles contain every mark of genuine mysticism, they lend no support to the contention that in view of his statement about knowing Christ no more after the flesh (2 Co 5^{16}) he underrates the importance of the Jesus of history and of His death upon the Cross. The idea of rising beyond Christ to pure absorption in the Absolute is quite foreign to the apostle's teaching. Nor is it to be forgotten that his point of view with reference to the external aspects of religion is simply that of opposition to the degenerate Judaism of his time. In his belittling of mere ceremonial he is a veritable mystic.

Not without justification, Plato has been generally regarded as " the father of European Mysticism." Ever

since at Athens about 388 B.C. he founded the famous
Academy, his name has been intimately connected with the
development of philosophic thought. All who have turned
their attention to speculative subjects have been obliged
to reckon with him.[1] His oral teaching took the form of the
Socratic dialogue, and this is also retained in his written
works, in certain of the later of which especially the speculative interest predominates. Gradually he developed his
central theory of Ideas, drawing a sharp distinction between
the conceptual world of ideas and that of sense perception.
Briefly his proposition is that whereas in the latter we are
in the region of ever-shifting phenomena, in the former we
are in contact with the true realities through which a single
purpose runs. Since first formulated, this great Platonic
principle has been of basic value for speculative philosophy,
mysticism included.

Philo, partly contemporary with Jesus and Paul, is the
chief representative of the Alexandrian movement toward
the amalgamation of Jewish monotheism and Greek
philosophy. Though intensely Platonic, he was loyal to
the substance of the Hebrew faith, and maintained that in
the Mosaic law was contained the entire content of religious
truth, whatever truth was taught in Greek philosophy
having been drawn from this source. The Greek poets and
philosophers he regarded as but " broken lights " of Moses.
From them, however, he took over the allegorical method,
and applied it extravagantly to the interpretation of
Scripture so as to evaporate its historical element and
bring it into line with his own theories. But while his
method enabled him to base religious life on the sacred
writings without being bound to the conceptions of an
earlier age, he was handicapped in his attempt to find a
synthesis between Hebraism and Hellenism by the fact that
there was a radical difference between these two modes
of thought, the one being that of intuition and the other
that of analysis. The influence of Plato on Philo's thought

---

[1] This is fitly set forth in one striking tribute :

> Thou wert the morning star among the living
>   Ere thy fair light had fled.
> Now having died thou art as Hesperus giving
>   New splendour to the dead.
>   —*Plato*, in Shelley's translation.

is very evident both in his abstract conception of God as merely a transcendent Being of whose nature nothing is to be known, and in his doctrine of the Logos, which has been aptly described as " a theistical transformation of the Platonic world of ideas." But although his doctrine of the Logos as a Divine intermediary between God and the world —albeit only in a half-personal way as a second principle— is the most distinctive feature in the teaching of Philo,[1] the main influence upon his writings from the Grecian side appears in a decidedly mystical strain in which there is a toning down of the severity both of the Jewish idea of God and of the moral code of the OT. Nor does Philo stop at this : he represents the height of human blessedness as a state of elevated abstraction in which even in this life a truly virtuous soul may rise to the vision of Deity. In this ecstatic experience man's reason is suspended ; he is merely as a stringed instrument played upon by the Spirit of God. Thus also of prophetic inspiration he says : " A prophet reveals nothing at all of his own, but is an interpreter, another suggesting all he utters, and he being in ignorance so long as he is in the ecstatic state. His reason having removed and withdrawn, the Divine Spirit visits and inhabits the citadel of the soul. The Spirit plays upon the organic structure of the voice, and brings to clear, vocal expression the things of which he prophesies " (*De Spec. Leg.*).

Philo's influence is reflected in the writings of the devout Plutarch (*c*. A.D. 40– ?), who is acquainted with the doctrine of the Logos, and in Greek philosophers like Apollonius of Tyana (*ob*. A.D. 96), who emphasizes the importance of the ecstatic vision. The Christian Platonists of Alexandria, too, notably Clement (*c*. 150–220), and Origen (*c*. 185–254), shewed sympathy with the mystical standpoint. If they never surrendered the claims of reason, they dealt largely in symbolism and allegory, distinguished between the faith of the ordinary believer and the gnosis or perfect knowledge of the completely instructed disciple, and advocated the reserva-

---

[1] Some scholars are of opinion that the Johannine doctrine of the Logos was taken over from Philo. So, *e.g.* Siegfried in his *Philo von Alexandria*. Harnack, on the other hand, holds that it is " essentially not that of Philo," and with this Zöckler agrees.

tion of the Christian mysteries for the enlightened.[1] The
general body of the pupils at the Catechetical School
were fed on " milk," the " meat " of mystic contemplation
being given only to those in the higher grades.   And thus
both by pagan and Christian writers the lead of Philo was
followed up until the Neoplatonic school, founded by
Ammonius Saccas (c. A.D. 175–245), reached its culminating
points in the systematic theosophy of the great Plotinus
(c. A.D. 205–270), who shared with Epictetus and Marcus
Aurelius the distinction of making the earliest approach
to Christianity on the part of pagan teachers.

Plotinus has been justly called " the mystic *par excellence*," in view of the fact that his mysticism marks the
final stage in the development of Greek philosophy.
Neoplatonism, of which he is the leading exponent, and
in which Mysticism received its first outstanding philosophical expression, has its root principle in the transcendence of the Deity, and proclaims as its goal the
direct apprehension of the Divine Essence.   According to
Plotinus, God and the world cannot be thought of together,
since the religious consciousness excludes all other.   The
eternal and absolute unity is viewed as the negation of all
things other than itself, the ideal being to shut out the
external world and to be filled with God alone.   It is
" the flight of the alone to the Alone."   In order to ascend
to the Divine unity, the mystic parts with everything that
is material, and retains no positive attribute which could
be ascribed to it.   It is unknowable, and therefore unspeakable.   We can only speak *about* it ; in itself it is
inexpressible.   Plotinus holds that the soul has a lower
aspect and a higher, the lower that of the animal life with
its desires and passions, and the higher, which, while
united to the body, differs from the Divine only by its
possession of " memory, imagination . . . and a finite
will."   In the apprehension of the Divine thought must
give way to vision, and this can be experienced only in rare

[1] These, however, differed essentially from those of the Mystery
Religions.   In chs. i. and ii. of his *Exhortation to the Heathen* Clement
scathingly condemns the monstrous impiety, absurdity, and
licentiousness of " the Mysteries of Idolatry " (those of Demeter,
Dionysus, Attis and Cybele and the Corybantes, etc.).   In his
eyes they are a " seed of evil and ruin."   " These mysteries," he
says, " are in short murders and funerals."

moments when the human spirit has cut itself adrift
from all finite conditions and even from conscious intelligence. We have it on the authority of his pupil
Porphyry that Plotinus reached the ecstatic vision of the
Absolute One only four times within six years. This
condition, it will be observed, involves the abandonment
of reason and self-consciousness—that is, it demands a
faculty above reason, by which subject and object are no
longer distinguishable, and life is confined to a mere
passive and transitory experience. In its later phases,
as represented first by Porphyry (A.D. 233–? 305) and
Jamblichus (ob. before A.D. 233), and then by the venerated
Proclus (A.D. 412–485) and his followers, Greek philosophy
degenerated into an amalgam of polytheism, theosophy,
theurgic rites, mysteries, and magical charms, no longer
aiming at the acquisition of knowledge, but simply at
popularizing the Neoplatonic system so as to facilitate
its practical application. In short, the philosophy of
Plotinus was developed only on its lower side.

In the contemplative and mystically coloured ascetism
of the Judæan Essenes who originated as early as the
second century B.C., we see reflected the general feeling
of hopeless dejection which characterized the age, combined with an eager yearning for Divine illumination. The
Essenes, who resided mainly in the vicinity of the Dead
Sea, formed an esoteric brotherhood based upon the ideal
of a simple life, together with the observance of a strict
morality and the cultivation of an apocalyptic gnosis and
of real fellowship with God. Their theology exhibits
a curious mixture of Jewish and foreign elements. While
practising a meticulous legalism, they shunned animal
sacrifices; they believed in immortality, but not in a
bodily resurrection; they paid much regard to angels,
whose names they professed to know, but would not
divulge; and it was customary for them at dawn to
turn in prayer towards the sun.

Later on, Alexandria became a centre of Christian
Mysticism both on its speculative and practical sides.
The pseudo-Dionysian writings, representing a mixture of
Christian and Neoplatonic doctrines, and containing a
far from negligible element of notions borrowed from the
religious philosophies of the Orient, combined with the

extensive introduction of monasticism to accelerate the
spread of the mystical movement. By Dionysius, who,
though posing as the Areopagite of Ac 17[34], seems to have
been a Syrian monk writing at a much later date, it is held
that all things proceed from and return to God ; that the
world is evolved from the Son (= the Logos of John, the
Nous of Plotinus) ; that while the higher part of the soul
may directly behold the " Divine images," the lower part
cannot see them except through symbols ; that only by the
negative road of abstraction is it possible to ascend to
Deity ; that the mystic must leave behind all things, both
in the sensible and in the intelligible worlds, till he enters
into the darkness of nescience that is truly mystical ; and
that evil is merely misplaced good. Besides, then, being a
pantheistic mystic after the Oriental pattern, Dionysius
represents a Buddhistic nihilism. In his view the external
world has no reality ; " our highest knowledge of God
consists in mystic ignorance " ; and passive absorption
in the " Divine Dark " to the extinction of human personality is the supreme end to be attained. Absolute
truth can be reached only by the way of entire negation,
and God by reason of His very excellence may well be
called Nothing. " The cause of all things," he writes, " is
neither soul nor intellect ; nor has it imagination, opinion, or
reason, or intelligence ; nor is it reason or intelligence ;
nor is it spoken or thought. It is neither number, nor
order, nor magnitude, nor littleness, nor equality, nor
inequality, nor similarity, nor dissimilarity. It neither
stands, nor moves, nor rests. . . . It is neither essence,
nor eternity, nor time. Even intellectual contact does
not belong to it. It is neither science nor truth. It is
not even royalty or wisdom ; not one ; not unity ; not
divinity or goodness, nor even spirit as we know it." For
the mystic in general who aspires to union with the
Absolute the *Via Negativa* is hard as he pursues it along
the purgative and illuminative steps by which he hopes
to reach the unitive heights. Roughly, the Christian
mystic draws the same distinction between the stages of
his upward progress, but in all cases alike it is unsatis-
factorily vague, and only partly true.

In the East, Mysticism was the natural accompaniment
of the prevailing philosophic doctrines. That the material

world is only an apparent reality was a view common to both the pantheistic Brahman and the Buddhistic nihilist. Numerous devotees gave themselves to silent contemplation ; others, to constrained bodily postures (standing on the head, etc.), and to various forms of self-torture, as conducive to saintliness and ultimate participation in Deity. All this was, in fact, a war against individual human personality, which melted away in the mystical absorption thus pursued as the highest soul. " The nearer nothing," says Angelus Silesius, " so much more divine."

It was presumably towards the close of the fifth century (according to Harnack the second half of the fourth century), when the candle of the pagan philosophy was flickering out in the Athenian schools, that the speculative mysticism of Neoplatonism was infused into Christian theology through the spurious compositions of the pretended Areopagite. Apparently the Church considered its position so secure as to feel no alarm at the mystical interpretation given to its creed by this unknown writer. Yet his bold transformation of the teaching of Proclus into a negative system of esoteric theology in which God, stripped of every positive attribute, becomes the nameless One and at the same time the completion of all things in the sense of 1 Co 15^{34}, introduced an element of subtle antagonism into an ostensibly co-operative movement. It was like a snake in the grass, and soon there was developed a keen conflict between the Church and Neoplatonism such as Kingsley has so graphically described in his *Hypatia*.

By the light which it threw upon the great problems raised by philosophy regarding God, the world, and the human soul, Christianity had awakened the dormant spiritual sense in vast multitudes of men. But in the matter of satisfying the spiritual needs of humanity it found a rival claimant in Neoplatonism, which took for its religious ideal the direct apprehension of the Divine Essence. Thus, is was believed, would the traditional worship receive a new impetus, and the desideratum, for want of which men were seceding to Christianity, be supplied. As I have stated elsewhere,[1] the promoters of

[1] Origen in *The World's Epoch-Makers*, p. 23.

Neoplatonism saw that if heathenism was to prevail, it must both get rid of its most glaring absurdities, and also strengthen itself by a large accession of ideas, principles, and rites. Thus they borrowed whatever appeared to them good from every available source. They contemplated nothing less than the introduction of a universal religion, constructed on principles so broad that the wise of all the earth could adhere to it. It was their aim to set matters right between philosophy and theology, between doctrine and life, and to satisfy the needs of the soul on a scale to which Christianity could make no pretension. Such was the situation which even Clement had already had to meet, and it fully explains the apologetic drift of his writings as well as his constant references to philosophy.

" The divine philosopher," Maximus the Confessor (580–622), a subtle, ascetic, and mystic monk, and a strenuous opponent of the Monothelites, marks the transition between Dionysius, on whose works he comments, and Scotus Erigena. In his theology he resembles Origen rather than Augustine. He uses the allegorical method of the Alexandrian school, and in his various works, particularly those relating to Christology, acquits himself as the last notable theologian of the Greek Church. As late as the fourteenth century, however, there appeared in Nicolaus Cabasilas, Bishop of Thessalonica, an independent mystic of the Greek Church, whose principal work, *Concerning the Life in Christ*, is worthy of special mention. It was translated into Latin, and for long was widely read. A critical edition of the Greek text by Gass was issued in 1849. The Bishop's somewhat ascetic but deeply spiritual mysticism exhibits a strong antipathy to the idea of justification by works, and to the outward ceremonialism practised in the Roman Church.

To the ninth century has to be ascribed the rise of Persian Sūfism, a form of pantheistic mysticism adopted by Mohammedans as a protest against the rigid monotheism, formal scholasticism, and tedious ritual of Islam. Under the successors of Mohammed, Persia had been conquered in the seventh century and the Koran forced upon its people, but they still cherished the traditional lore of Zoroaster. In particular they shewed an ardent devotion, and aimed at a self-denying and disinterested love. The best Persian poetry is permeated by this species of mysticism, in which a keen sense of the pantheistic unity of all things lent additional zest to the enjoyment of the beautiful, alike in nature and in man. The writers find their main inspiration in women and wine, and Mohammedan theologians contrive to interpret mystically even their most licentious strains. Sensual amours are made to typify the joys of union with the Divine ; the tavern, an oratory ; and intoxication, the amazement of the astounding vision and insensibility to all earthly thoughts. However, in certain pantheistic poems of Hafiz, Saadi, and others, a directly religious motive is present, and the ardent longing of the soul to flee away from all worldly enjoyments, to immerse itself in Deity, and to realize its ideal of rest, finds pointed utterance. The tendencies in mysticism of this sort were not all good, but neither were they all evil. For the Sūfi, we are told, " when the mystery of the essence of being has been revealed to him, the furnace of the world becomes transformed into a garden of flowers," so that " the adept sees the almond through the envelope of its shell, and, no longer beholding himself, perceives only his Friend ; in all that he sees, beholding his face, in every atom perceiving the whole." [1]

It seems probable that Hindu influences are to be associated with the introduction of Sūfism into Islam, and later at all events it developed into a mystic pantheism which combined the teaching of Zoroaster with that of Buddha ; but as it was, like that of the Essenes, virtually a secret cult, comparatively little is known concerning it. Personal testimonies and experiences on the part of its adherents are rarely recorded. In a lengthy quotation from a French translation of part of the autobiography of Al-Ghazzali, a celebrated Moslem doctor of the eleventh century, Dr. James, however, has opened a window through which to some extent we can scan the religious features of Sūfism. According to this writer, " The science of the Sūfis aims at detaching the heart from all that is not God, and at giving it for sole occupation the meditation of the Divine Being. I read until I understood all

[1] 'Attar, *The Seven Valleys*, quoted by E. Underhill, *The Mystic Way*, p. 51.

2

that can be learned by study and hearsay. Then I recognized that what pertains most exclusively to their
method is just what no study can grasp, but only transport, ecstasy, and the transformation of the soul. . . .
I went to Syria, where I remained about two years, with
no other occupation than living in retreat and solitude,
conquering my desires, combating my passions, training
myself to purify my soul, to make my character perfect,
to prepare my heart for meditating on God—all according
to the methods of the Sūfis, as I had read of them."   For
ten years more he struggled on in the hope of attaining
the state of ecstasy, but never found it except for a few
single hours. " During this solitary state," he says,
" things were revealed to me which it is impossible either
to describe or to point out. I recognized for certain that
the Sūfis are assuredly walking in the path of God. The
next key of the contemplative life consists in the humble
prayers which escape from the fervent soul, and in the
meditations on God in which the heart is swallowed up
entirely. But in reality this is only the beginning of the
Sūfi life, the end of Sūfism being total absorption in God.
The chief properties of prophetism are perceptible only
during the transport, by those who embrace the Sūfi life.
The prophet is endowed with qualities to which you
possess nothing analogous, and which consequently you
cannot possibly understand. . . . But the transport which
one attains by the method of the Sūfis is like an immediate
perception, as if one touched the object with one's hand." [1]

As in Mysticism generally, the ecstatic transport experienced by the individual cannot be communicated to any
other.

[1] A. Schmölders : *Essai sur les écoles philosophiques chez les Arabes*,
Paris, 1842, pp. 54–68, abridged ; quoted by James, *op. cit.* p. 402 ff.

PART II

SPREAD OF CHRISTIAN MYSTICISM IN THE WEST

1. *Until the End of the Thirteenth Century.*

THE first Latin propagandist of Christian mysticism was Victorinus, a convert from Neoplatonism (*c.* A.D. 360). He speaks mystically of Christ and the Church, declaring that " the Church is Christ," that as presented in the sacramental bread " the body of Christ is life," and that " the resurrection of Christ is our resurrection."

It was chiefly through Augustinian Platonism that Mysticism was introduced into Christian theology in Latin countries ; yet Augustine himself can only to a very limited extent be reckoned a mystic. The bulk of his teaching has no relation to mysticism, but his modified Platonism rendered him sympathetic towards it. As Eucken observes, " Such men as Plotinus and Augustine . . . made accessible to man a new world of pure inwardness," in which all anxieties of soul are " changed into an intuitive vision of Eternal Truth, and into the worship of Infinite Love," conformably to Augustine's own great saying : " Thou hast created us for Thyself, and our heart is not at rest until it rests in Thee." While not identifying God with the world, he was filled with a sense of His beauty, and was perhaps led by the Neoplatonic doctrine concerning the relation of individual souls to the World-Soul to arrive at his own conclusion with respect to the mystical union of the Christian with Christ.

From the time of the Pseudo-Dionysius the centre of interest as regards Christian mysticism is no longer found in the East, but in the West. John Scotus Erigena (ninth century) fused the Dionysian speculation into a coherent system nearly allied to Neoplatonism, and greatly influenced mediæval mysticism both on its scholastic and

on its mystical sides. He translated into Latin the
writings of Dionysius, together with the *Scholia* of Maximus,
and made their system the groundwork of his own. To
him we owe the dictum that every creature, visible
and invisible, is a theophany or manifestation of God.
On this principle as set forth in his *De Divisione Naturæ*
natural objects are types of spiritual truths, and the very
acme of created things is the soul of man untarnished by
sin. As nothing can be predicated of God, He may
rightly be called Nothing. From this incomprehensible
essence eternally proceeds the world of ideas or the Word
of God in whom all things subsist. With reference to the
great problem of the age, namely, the relation of God to the
world, he views Him as the beginning of all things, and
His will as an unknowable enigma. Although he asserts
that sacrifice is only metaphorically true, and that man's
will is a mere capitulation to the external authority of the
Church, mysticism, so far as represented by him, offers
no opposition to the ecclesiastical dogma which as a whole
is wrapped up in the philosophic garment in which it is
clothed. John Scotus was a boldly speculative thinker,
and stronger on the intellectual than on the pietistic or
practical side. Affirming that true philosophy is true
religion, and that true religion is true philosophy, he is
chiefly concerned to maintain the transcendence in contrast to the immanence of God, and apart from the Neoplatonic strain in his writings can scarcely be classed as a
mystic at all. His heterodox teaching, in which the spirit
of Origen reappears, was opposed to the doctrine of pre-
destination and to the idea of punishment on the part of
God. It met with a surprising measure of toleration until
his writings were expressly banned at a synod held at Paris
in 1209.

After Augustine, Anselm (1033–1109) was considered
the brightest star of the Western Church. Of Italian
origin, and of a studious disposition, he (in 1060) entered
the monastery of Bec, of which he became first prior and
then abbot. In 1093 he was appointed Archbishop of
Canterbury, and strenuously resisted the attempted
subjection of the Church to the temporal power. Theologically, he was the father of orthodox scholasticism.
Viewing the dogmas of the Church as of equal authority

with revelation itself, he held that the truths of Christianity must be received in faith, and that the function of reason is merely to help us to understand what we believe. His teaching was thus diametrically opposed to that of Erigena, according to whom religion is scarcely more than practical philosophy. His most famous work is that on the Incarnation (*Cur Deus homo*), in which he seeks philosophically to establish the doctrine of a vicarious Atonement. A man of the highest character as well as of striking intellectual power, Anselm's deepest interest was the culture of heart-religion. His dialectics never dulled his keen practical piety or the ardour of his Christian feeling, to which he gives glowing expression in his *Meditations and Prayers*. These entitle him to a certain rank among the mystics; but as Dr. A. C. Welch has said, " his piety has a chaste reverence even when it is most fervid. There does not appear the recoil from blank despair to morbid ecstasy. . . . And there is an ethical strain in the work which gives vitality to the most passionate devotion." [1]

Influenced by the writings of the pseudo-Dionysius and of Erigena, Amalric of Bena, a teacher at Paris about the end of the twelfth century (*ob.* 1207), founded a distinctive group of rationalistic and pantheistic mystics in direct antagonism to the Church. They denied the reality of matter and the resurrection of the body, and maintained the identity of man with God, as well as the needlessness of sacraments. Developing a decided antinomianism amounting to an utter perversion of genuine mysticism, they taught the dangerous doctrine that to live in love is to be immune from evil. Peculiar to them also was the form in which they held the doctrine of a historically progressive revelation. The period from Abraham to Christ they viewed as the age of the Father; that from Christ to their own time as the age of the Son; and their own time (1260 onwards) as the age of the Spirit. Many of them renounced all outward worship and stigmatized the Pope as Antichrist. Among other and more degenerate aspects of mediæval Mysticism were the apocalyptic, represented by Joachim of Floris; the blatantly pantheistic, professed by the Brethren of the

[1] *Anselm and his Work*, p. 58 f.

Free Spirit, who repudiated the moral law as well as the Church, having, they said, no more need of either, and whose adherents were largely massed in the Rhineland and formed a close connexion with the Beghards and Béguines (associations of men and women respectively) of the Low Countries ; and the severely ascetic, according to which the gospel is to be only symbolically understood, and the collective Roman priesthood viewed as devotees of the devil. The last-named sectaries headed by Ortlieb of Strassburg, were akin to the Cathari (= Puritans), a gnostic fraternity originating in the Balkans in the eleventh, and spreading widely over Europe until the thirteenth, century. Doctrinally, they adopted a course dualism, asserting that matter is intrinsically evil, and busied themselves with metaphysical speculations concerning its nature and origin.

It was no easy task for the Church to check these doctrinal aberrations while at the same time careful to foster mystical enthusiasm, but some notable men gave themselves to this task. Among these was Bernard, abbot of Clairvaux (1090–1153), founder of seventy monasteries, a great preacher and author of many beautiful hymns. He was also an unrivalled mediator in the principal disputes of his time, an orator who roused the zeal of Christendom for the second Crusade into the Holy Land, a fervid proclaimer of the love of God, and an unswerving believer in the power of prayer and in the presence of Christ as the true equipment for all his work. Bernard's practical mysticism was mainly concerned with the mode of arriving through asceticism at the knowledge and enjoyment of God. " As iron heated red-hot loses its own appearance and glows like fire, so (he says) must all human feeling towards the Holy One be wholly transfused into the will of God. For how shall God be all in all if anything of man remains in man ? The substance will indeed remain, but in another form, another glory, another power " (*De diligendo Deo*, chap. x.). At the Council of Sens (1140) Bernard was chosen to confront Abelard, the scholastic philosopher and theologian, who was charged with subordinating faith to reason and so leading his many pupils astray. The result was striking. Bernard entered into no argumentative discussion ; he merely quoted some passages from Abelard's writings, leaving him to vindicate them and the Council to decide. Disarmed by Bernard's simplicity, the brilliant Abelard, famed as the most distinguished teacher in Europe, was speechless, except to say, " I appeal to the Court of Rome." This apparently passing episode marked the first stage in the conflict between Scholasticism and Mysticism, which afterwards set in with continuous and increasing force. The significance of St. Bernard in the history of Mysticism lies in his devotional bent of mind, and hardly at all in speculative thought. He was primarily concerned to keep before men's minds the image of the crucified Jesus as the " Bridegroom of the soul." This is the burden of his hymns, and also of his remarkable commentaries on the *Song of Solomon*, in which, however, not the individual but the Church collectively is represented as the bride of Christ.

The condemnation of Abelard led to stricter adherence to the dogmatic standards of the Church. In the new school of St. Victor, a monastery at Paris, an effort was made to amalgamate Monasticism with Mysticism. Its founder was Hugo (*ob*. 1141), a friend of St. Bernard, and often spoken of as " another Augustine." Combining depth of thought with great erudition and warmth of heart, he left his mark on mediæval theology. In his writings Hugo avoided speculative extravagance, and, like Augustine, introduced a certain mystical strain into his teaching. With him it was a favourite maxim that in order to know God one must know himself, and also set a higher value upon purity of heart than upon philosophy. Peter the Lombard, from 1159 Bishop of Paris, formed a dialectically arranged compendium of doctrinal sayings of the Fathers, which, although modestly called by himself, " the widow's mite cast into the treasury of the Church," became the mediæval standard of orthodoxy. Lombardus nevertheless did not escape sharp criticism. His very project of attempting to present a combined view of patristic theories of revelation was a novelty fitted to arouse distrust. He still clung to the dialectic method, but under Hugo's successor, Richard of St. Victor, that school departed more and more from dialectics as too formal and arid in relation to the Christian life. Without undervaluing reason, Richard regarded suprarational ecstasy as the highest

state of the soul, and meanwhile through the joint influence
of Peter and Richard mysticism and scholasticism were
in a measure reconciled, the one taking on more of a
scientific definiteness, and the other occupying itself
mainly with the exposition of the dogmatic of the Church.
But in 1180, Walter, the next abbot of St. Victor, brought
against the Lombard a charge of Nihilism in respect of
his teaching that our Lord's human body was impersonal
(" Quod Christus non sit aliquid, secundum quod est
homo "), so that in that respect He was not an individual.

Before the second half of the thirteenth century the
speculative spirit began to predominate among the schoolmen. The explanation and defence of Church dogma was
based more upon the Aristotelian philosophy than upon
Scripture, the truth of which it professed to prove and
illustrate. At the same time there were many scholastic
mystics who were not satisfied with mere philosophical
argument. These advocated inward recollection and contemplation inspired by self-sacrifice and the love of God
as essential to the real perception and enjoyment of Divine
truth. In their view this aspect of theology also called
for scientific expression. Such a combination of dialectics
and mysticism found a prominent representative in Bonaventura, who, in 1256, became general of the Franciscans,
as Thomas Aquinas already was of the Dominicans. At
once philosopher and divine, he taught both the transcendence and immanence of God. He was made Bishop of
Albano, and was created Cardinal in 1273, the year before
his death. Known as " the seraphic doctor," he mingled
with his dialectics much that bore upon mystical and
practical piety. In his arrangement of the mental powers
he follows the Victorines, and designates the capacity for
mystic intuition as " scintilla " and " apex mentis," while
using a multiplicity of phrases descriptive of the union
with God. Dante in Canto XII of the *Paradiso* signifi-
cantly makes Bonaventura sing the praises of St. Dominic
in return for the eulogy of St. Francis by Aquinas, to shew
that in Heaven's pure light all party spirit is dissolved,
and that the rival leaders were both pillars of the Church,
and indeed it is only just to recognize that both of these
schoolmen were truly saintly souls :

For to one end each laboured from his birth.

The learned Roger Bacon (1214–94), a brilliant teacher of Oxford and a Franciscan monk, exposed the defects of scholasticism, and urged the necessity of studying the Scriptures in the original Hebrew and Greek. His aim was to counteract the influence of Peter the Lombard, whose " Sentences " were in general use as a text-book in the theological faculties in the universities, to the practical exclusion of Scripture itself. " The text," he says, " is subjected to the magisterial summary alone." Accused of heresy, Bacon experienced a long imprisonment until released by Clement IV, who, when legate to England, had known and highly esteemed him. Early in the twelfth century, Rupert, abbot of Deutz, had previously emphasized the need for Bible study, but in his commentaries forsook the literal interpretation of the text for the devious ways of allegorism.

Albertus Magnus, Dominican teacher at Paris and Cologne, and afterwards Archbishop of Ratisbon (1260–80), was the foremost scholar of his time, and known as " the universal doctor." Owing to his vast knowledge of science, he was generally accounted a wizard. In keenness of intellect, however, he did not excel, and in his prelections and writings he brought Scripture too little into contribution ; but running through his scholasticism there was a decidedly mystical vein. Concerning the true mode of attaining to union with God he writes : " Nothing pleases God more than a mind free from all occupation and distractions. Sense and imagination cannot bring us to Him, but only the desire of a pure heart. Do not think about the world, nor about thy friends, nor about the past, present, or future ; but consider thyself to be out of the world and alone with God, as if thy soul were already separated from the body, and had no longer any interest in peace or war, or the state of the world." [1] In this we have a good example of " the negative way."

Thomas Aquinas (c. 1226–74), a Dominican and a pupil of Albertus Magnus, familiarly known as " the angelic doctor," became second master at Cologne. Through his action in concert with the Franciscan General, Bonaventura, the mendicant orders were able to triumph over their leading assailant, William of St. Amour, and in 1272

[1] Quoted by W. R. Inge, op. cit. p. 145.

Aquinas got a professorship in Naples. Modestly refusing proffered ecclesiastical promotion, he died while on his way to attend at the papal behest a Council at Lyons in 1204, the year which also witnessed Bonaventura's decease. Aquinas is best known as the author of the *Summa Theologica*, which still ranks as an authoritative statement of Roman Catholic doctrine. Under the three categories of God, Man, and the God-man, he treats on a grand scale of the fusion of theology and philosophy as embracing the entire circuit of human knowledge. It was the aim of Aquinas to show that natural and supernatural knowledge are not in reality antagonistic, but complementary parts of truth, which is one and indivisible. Both external nature and the truth contained in the Christian evangel are regarded as merely different aspects of God's revelation of Himself to man.

The views expressed in this important treatise were strongly opposed by Duns Scotus (*ob.* 1308), the British Franciscan doctor, a man of keen intellect and deep learning, who, taking as his basic principle the independence of the will, and not, like Aquinas, the intellect, accentuated the contrast between faith and reason, and gave to theology a predominantly practical instead of a strictly theoretical aspect. In the work of Aquinas scholasticism had reached its zenith, and there was now inaugurated a new period in which his fame began to be shared with Duns Scotus, " the subtle doctor." The ideas of these two masters became the watchwords of their respective orders, the Dominicans being designated Thomists and the Franciscans Scotists. In philosophy the Dominicans were Aristotelians and Nominalists. Theologically, they were orthodox Churchmen, while the Scotists shewed a rationalistic tendency. In gauging the relations between the two parties it must not be forgotten that some scholastics were likewise mystics, and that some mystics were strict logicians. The mystic tendency is very discernible in Aquinas himself, and Bonaventura made considerable use of the scholastic method. At this stage in our survey it must be clearly understood that for the most part the mystics latterly abandoned metaphysics altogether, and contented themselves with cultivating theology from the devotional and ascetic standpoint. They repudiated the scholastic view that religion is something external to the mind. There still remained, however, prominent representatives of the scholastic tendency of whom it is necessary to take account.

2. *From the Fourteenth Century until the Reformation.*

Among speculative mystics none ranks higher than Henry (commonly called " Meister ") Eckhart (*c.* 1260–1329), a popular Dominican preacher, who became vicar-general of the Order in 1307.   On account of his alleged complicity with the Beghards and Brethren of the Free Spirit—sects somewhat akin to the Quakers—his teaching was impugned by the Dominican General, and by the Archbishop of Cologne, who singled out from his writings twenty-eight statements for censure.   Although Eckhart had no external connexion with the " Brethren," and declared his loyalty to Church doctrine, the accusation against him in respect of seventeen counts of the libel was sustained by the Pope, and a Bull of condemnation, suppressing his tractates and affirming that he had recanted, was issued in 1329, just after his death.   Whatever were his relations with the Brethren of the Free Spirit, he certainly had no part in their antinomian views and practices.   It was still the object of Eckhart to effect a compromise between the two opposing schools of religious thought.   While seeking dialectically to analyse and develop Christian dogmas, he was at the same time alive to the need for inward contemplation.   The problem was to do justice alike to the intellect and to the feelings, to arrive in short at a speculative basis for Church dogmatic compatible with a practical religious mysticism capable of satisfying the deepest yearnings of the soul.   Eckhart wrote in German for the people, and the lack of qualifying phrases in his various writings tended to expose him to the charge of heresy.   He had read widely from Augustine downwards, and he so often quotes from " a master " who is evidently Aquinas, as to call forth the unfair opinion that everything in Eckhart is contained in the *Summa*. His bold speculation led him to the brink, and actually over the brink, of pantheism.   Although he distinguishes between God and the creature, he views Nature as " the

lower part of the Godhead," and it is even a more harmful
aspect of his teaching that it points to the deification of
man as the goal to be eagerly sought. There is, he holds,
an uncreated Godlike element in the soul, "a spark"
(*Funken*) or light of the Spirit, which must detach itself
from the finite after the pattern of Christ, that through
contemplation of God men may, like Him, become sons of
God, and persons even as He is a Person. According to
Eckhart, there is no subordination of the Son to the
Father ; the generation of the Son is eternal, and the
union of the Father and the Son is effected through the
Holy Spirit. Our personality is, however, distinct from
that of God, and the knowledge of Him which is mediated
by Christ requires to be supplemented by reason, which
"presses ever upwards." For him the Trinity is not an
emanation of the Absolute ; rather are the three Persons
essentially inherent in the Godhead. Moral evil is the
assertion of self-will, and the attempt to be or do something outside of God. Eckhart avoids the elaboration
of scales of ascent and lists of mental states and virtues
formulated by many previous mystical theologians.
Among other features characteristic of him are his indifference to the historical ; his view of hell, purgatory,
and paradise, as not localities but states ; and his insistence that perfect love is not contingent upon the hope
of recompense. In his writings we breathe an atmosphere
other than that of the churchly mystics. While giving
full weight to the systematized dogma of the Church, he
contrives by the unrestricted use of reason to reduce the
historical facts of Christianity to an idealistic or mythical
expression of truth that lies within the scope of human
reason. His system is marked by a peculiar blend of
intellect and religious feeling, and notwithstanding his
bold identification of the human and the divine, it cannot
be doubted that he everywhere manifests a truly devout
and Christian spirit. Noteworthy also is his vacillation
between monkish mediævalism and the spirit of modern
Christianity. On the one hand we see in him an ascetic
in the enjoyment of fellowship with God, and on the other
a reformer at war with the veneration of saints' relics and
all outward badges affected by professing Christians.
Eckhart's influence in Church history is thus the water-

shed of two different streams of thought. Known and
esteemed in his day as the master " from whom God
concealed nothing," he stands at the meeting-point of
mediæval monasticism and German metaphysical theology.

In 1330, Nicolas of Bâle, a wealthy layman, formed a
mystic brotherhood styled " the Friends of God." The
society included many devout women, especially in the
converts which with the aid of Elizabeth of Thüringen had
sprung up in the preceding century. To it belonged the
notable Mechtildis of Magdeburg (1214–77), whose work,
Das fliessende Licht der Gottheit, reveals familiarity with
The Eternal Gospel of Joachim of Floris. Close connexion
between the Friends was kept up by correspondence and
frequent visitation. Though they attended the Church
services, they lamented its decay, and desiderated a warmer
and more practical type of piety. Strongly condemning the
vices of the age, they preached the need of repentance and
holy living. In spite of the hostility of the Inquisition they
went to and fro ministering to their secret adherents.
Allegorists in their interpretation of Scripture, they
practised an ascetic mysticism, greatly affected visions
and revelations, and urged absolute submission to the will
of God. Apart from his speculative theology, they were in
many respects akin to Eckhart.

Prominent among these was Henry Suso (1295–1365), a
Dominican of Ulm. Though an ardent follower of Eckhart,
he represents a type of mysticism more imaginative and
poetical than that of his master. His impulse towards
extreme asceticism is evident from details furnished in his
autobiography, such as the following : Writing in the
third person, he says : " He wore for a long time a hair
shirt and an iron chain, until the blood ran from him.
In the undergarment he had strips of leather fixed, into
which a hundred and fifty brass nails, pointed and filed
sharp were driven, and the points of the nails were always
turned towards the flesh. In this he used to sleep at
night . . . tormented also by noxious insects. . . . He
devised something further—two leathern loops into which
he put his hands, and fastened one on each side his throat,
and made the fastenings so secure that even if his cell
had been on fire about him he could not have helped
himself. After some twenty years of this tormenting

exercise, he saw in vision a messenger from heaven, who told him that God required this of him no longer. Whereupon he discontinued it." He then entered on a new phase of suffering. Instead of self-imposed tortures he was now to experience those inflicted by persecutors, robbers, and false accusers. In 1340 he became a popular if visionary preacher, gained many converts, and pled for complete resignation to the Divine will. His main work is his *Book of Eternal Wisdom* (1338), which takes the form of an imaginary conversation between the Saviour and His servant, with special reference to His passion. Suso's principal contention is that redemption means emancipation from the form of the creature, renewal in the likeness of Christ, and transformation into the Godhead. Dr. Inge describes this book as " a prose poem of great beauty," and its author has also been designated " the minnesinger of the love of God." Towards the end of his career, Suso dictated a history of his life, which is unique in respect of its full and frank expression of his mystical experiences and its vivid human interest. While his writings are not free from a pantheistic tendency, he never wavers in his earnest desire for the salvation of sinful men.

John Tauler (1300–61), a Dominican priest, called by Melanchthon the German Origen, ranks high among the mystics of his time. The beginning of his real religious life he attributes to the effect produced on him by Nicolas of Bâle, who, after listening to his preaching, frankly told him that he was " suffering himself to be killed by the letter," and that at all hazards he must renounce the pride of reason, and in utter abasement and self-surrender take up his cross and follow Christ. From Strassburg, where in spite of the papal interdict of 1324 he was at first allowed to perform his official duties, he was compelled to flee to Bâle, the chief stronghold of the " Friends of God." Returning to Strassburg, he bore himself heroically during the plague of 1348, and till his death preached to large enthusiastic audiences. More books have been written about him than he ever wrote himself. He was the author of a few short treatises, but is known mainly by his sermons, which appeared in various editions and dialects and reveal his familiarity with the mystics who preceded him. His preaching appealed to men of every class, and won for him the title of the " enlightened doctor." For the most part his teaching coincided with that of Eckhart, but on some important points he differed from him. Instead of Eckhart's " spark " he speaks of " the uncreated ground of the soul," which influences us not directly, as that writer asserts, but through the medium of " the created ground." Other points of contrast are that he is less speculative and less pantheistic, but more deeply imbued with the sense of sin and more devotional than Eckhart. Through his sermons, conceived in a markedly practical spirit and delivered in the German tongue, he gained power with the people and an influence surpassing that of any other mystical teacher of his day. He showed himself averse alike to the too obtrusive metaphysics of Eckhart and the fantastic extravagances of Suso, and expressly dissociated himself from the heretical aberrations of the Brethren of the Free Spirit and the Beghards. Besides being a great preacher, Tauler was a penetrative thinker. This appears, for example, in his view of the creation as the effect of an idea eternally existing in the mind of God and finding expression through the Trinity. In the mystic ascent to God he distinguishes three stages. The first is the practice of self-discipline ; the second, the contemplation of the image of our Lord leading to trans- formation into that image ; and the third, perfect sympathy with Christ, reached only gradually through the operation of the Divine Spirit. Although, like other mystics, he gives special prominence to the indwelling of Christ in the soul, he is not indifferent to the historical fact of His sacrifice on Calvary, or to the duty of making His earthly life our constant pattern. Tauler's claim that in the passive surrender of intellect and will, and absorption in the love of God, the spiritual life attains its highest reach, reflects the growing trend from speculative mysticism in the direction of quietism.

John of Ruysbroek (1292–1381), the leading Dutch mystic, after being for long vicar of St. Gudule's, Brussels, entered the neighbouring Augustine monastery of regular canons at Gröndal, of which he was prior until his death. Neither a learned nor a literary man, he was known as the " ecstatic doctor," on account of the importance he attached to the experience by which the soul, free from the shackles of outward sense, becomes immersed in the Divine love. Although clearly influenced by Eckhart, he sometimes cautiously avoids making use of his language. A severe critic of the Brethren of the Free Spirit, his mysticism takes on less of a speculative than of a practical complexion. As a tribute to the life of the community at Gröndal, the lay preacher, Gerald Groot (1340–84), at Deventer in the Netherlands, founded a Christian association, whose members took upon them no monastic vows or formal rules, but led a simple religious life in which, like the early disciples, "they had all things common." They demanded that preaching should everywhere be in the mother tongue. The well-known Thomas à Kempis was connected with this brotherhood. In his writings, which are not without the marks of talent, Ruysbroek deprecates all mere idle contemplation, and like Tauler lays stress upon the active will. It is noteworthy that he claims to have set down nothing except under the inspiration of the Holy Ghost. Yet Gerson (see below) declared against him, and branded his opinions as pantheistic. In his statements respecting the idea and course of deification he does indeed seem to be so carried away by his aspiration after union with God as virtually to overlook the vital distinction between the Creator and the creature. Apparently his aim was to hold the balance between the orthodox and the heterodox mystics, although the line of demarcation drawn by him is too thin to prevent misunderstanding.

A later name associated with scholastic mysticism is that of John Charlier de Gerson (1363–1429), a leading representative of "Gallicanism," which, though itself scholastic, opposed the barren subtleties of speculative philosophers. With a Nominalist philosophy he followed up the efforts of Bonaventura to remedy the antagonism between the speculative and the mystical theologians. A Chancellor of the University of Paris from 1392, he strove to purify the lives of the clergy through "a reformation of head and members," and at the long-drawn-out Council of Constance (1414–18) to put an end to the papal schism then devastating the Church. His object was to clear up the relation of the Church to the Pope, his great contention being that the Church Councils had an authority superior to that of " the Vicar of Christ," whom he boldly declared to be not infallible, but " a sinner and liable to sin."   The part he took in advocating the condemnation of John Hus remains a blot upon his record.   Distressed at the seeming hopelessness of the papal *impasse,* and owing to the hostility of the Duke of Burgundy, Gerson retired for a time to the Tyrol, and latterly entering a monastery at Lyons, there ended his days prosecuting his studies and teaching the young.   Without abandoning dialectic methods, Gerson in his treatise on *Mystical Theology* rejects individual speculation, and approves the type of mysticism inaugurated by St. Bernard and the Victorines, with its emphasis on the affections as well as the intellect.   He specially stresses the inward teaching by which God is experimentally made known to the devout soul.   Under the head of speculative mysticism he discusses questions of psychology ;   mystical theology he distinguishes as a theology of love.   Through love, God is apprehended, and through love the will is made subject to God's will.   Pierre D'Ailly (1350–1425) and Gerson were the last exponents of mysticism within the scholastic framework.

The most celebrated representative of purely mystical piety in later pre-Reformation times was Thomas à Kempis (1380–1471), vicar in Deventer, and afterwards one of the regular canons in the Augustine house of Mount St. Agnes, near Zwolle, in the Netherlands.   He is the reputed author of the world-famous work on *The Imitation of Christ.* In this little book, the title of which is strictly applicable to the opening chapter only, the writer minutely analyses the motives and feelings, makes love the test of good and evil, counsels the reader to keep his gaze fixed on Christ, and indicates the toilsome upward path of the individual soul in crushing the evil propensities of the natural man and working out its own salvation.   It gives due prominence to the Cross, and in beautiful language descants upon the virtues of humility and uprightness of heart. But after all it sets forth only a monkish Christianity. To the practical side of the Christian faith in relation to the duty which we owe to man the writer is apparently indifferent.   Notwithstanding his own declaration that " whosoever would fully and feelingly understand the words of Christ must endeavour to conform his life wholly to the

3

life of Christ," the example of Him who " went about
doing good " is not held up for imitation ; it is ignored.
Great, therefore, as has been its appeal to some felt need
of the Christian mind, this book cannot be regarded as a
satisfactory presentation of the Christian life in its fulness.

In 1516, shortly before his break with Rome, Luther
issued a little volume entitled *German Theology*, with a
preface of emphatic approval. " Next to the Bible and
St. Augustine," he said, " I do not know of any book
from which I have learned better what God, Christ, man,
and all things are." It bears internal evidence of being
the work of a priest in close association with the " Friends
of God." Its standpoint is largely that of Eckhart,[1]
Tauler, and Ruysbroek, but a more practical religious
direction is given to speculative mystic theology. The
extreme individualism of Thomas à Kempis is avoided,
and, in particular, self-sacrifice, or rising above the " I "
and " mine," is put forward as the prime necessity for
conformity to the will of God. Except in so far as it
shares the opinion so prevalent in the Middle Ages, that
the divine rises only upon the ruins of the earthly, this
short book still deservedly continues to be prized as a
gem amongst devotional writings.

From the developments of thought and religion in the
fourteenth and fifteenth centuries, certain conclusions
emerge :

(1) The decline of scholasticism and the independent
development of mysticism became more marked. The
mystic no longer sought the proof of Divine truth as
logically conceived in the harmonious co-operation of faith
and reason, but in direct fellowship with God through an
inner illumination of the soul. For him such an experience
brought greater enlightenment, peace, sanctifying power,
and assurance, than mere outward revelations or logical
reasoning could afford.

(2) The attempt to effect a compromise between Scholasticism and Mysticism was destined to end in failure,
partly because of the essential incompatibility between a

[1] It may be noted that according to this book the soul has two
eyes. The one sees into eternity ; the outlook of the other is
towards time and the cosmos. Apparently the " right eye "
corresponds to Eckhart's " spark."

fettered philosophy and a mysticism given over to blind acceptance of the negative way, partly because of the frequent overlapping of the two tendencies, and partly because of the decline of scholasticism, which gradually eliminated one of the parties concerned.

(3) Schoolmen and mystics alike helped to pave the way for the religious revolution that was near at hand. Though shorn of its power, and with fewer and fewer to do it reverence, though even the operation of a blood-transfusion of mysticism was repeatedly performed with a view to revivify its moribund condition, and nothing could avail to invest it with a new reality of living interest, yet it is not to be forgotten that scholasticism had been distinguished by a thirst for knowledge and a genuine spirit of scientific investigation. It had an outlook not confined to metaphysics and divinity, but extending to frank discussion of political and social questions as well. And in thus freely canvassing whatever was instinct with meaning for man, the scholastics opened the way for the debating of those great issues that were to end in the transformation not only of religion, but also of secular government and social well-being. As the late Professor Brewer has said, " The work of the Schoolman was accomplished. He had formed the mind of Christendom for the great events to come." The contribution of mysticism, which urged the necessity of a devotional and practical piety, was of equal and even greater importance in leading up to a real reformation. By its insistence on inward personal religion it restored to theology the very breath of life, which had been choked by the undue predominance of dialectic and philosophical speculation. While, however, mysticism rendered invaluable service to theology by thus counteracting the influence of a formal and metaphysical dialectic, it could not of itself produce a full reformation. At most it could supply an element indispensable to the completion of the edifice on which Luther and his associates were to place the copestone.

(4) Though during these two centuries the desire for reformation persisted, the true nature of religious reform was largely lost sight of. Attention was too exclusively directed to the removal of scandals ; the preaching of repentance was lacking. The essential element in a real

reformation, that of a new spirit, was overlooked. The Bohemian, John Hus, in basing salvation on faith in the crucified Jesus, pointed out the way, but at the Council of Constance (1415) he was most unjustly led to the stake. Instead of the sacrifice of a contrite heart, men thought only of an ecclesiastical reformation " in head and members," and even as regards this would take no action until the installation of a new pope.

Some notable mystical aberrations marked the eve of the Reformation. An evangelical mysticism was appreciated by Luther, but alongside of this there sprang up another and less worthy type of mysticism which was alien to the Church. A widespread Anabaptist movement, organized in Münster, was soon dissipated by internal discord and powerful opposition. Though still directed against all external Church forms, a better species of mysticism was that associated with Caspar Schwenkfeld (1490–1561), a nobleman of Silesia, who, after adhering to the Wittenberg Reformation, broke with the Lutherans, rejecting their views concerning the Eucharist, Scripture, and the human nature of Christ, in the interest of a purely inward Christianity similar to that favoured by the " Friends." A small remnant of this sect appears to be still extant. In the scholarly and versatile Agrippa of Nettesheim (*ob.* 1535), the grandiloquent author of *Occulta Philosophia*, the monks met with a keen and resolute adversary. He adhered, however, to the Catholic Church, and in this respect, as well as in the general trend of his mysticism, resembled his more famous contemporary the Swiss Paracelsus (1493–1541), who, after being two years professor of medicine at Bâle, was expelled from that office as " an egregious quack " vehemently opposed to Galen and other accepted authorities. With reference to this, and the strange magical antics to which he later on confessed, the poet Browning in his *Paracelsus* makes him say :

> They took revenge
> For past credulity in casting shame
> On my real knowledge.

For several years Paracelsus led a wandering life as a sort of mountebank, though often consulted by prominent personages anxious to avail themselves of his medical skill. Ultimately, under the wing of the archbishop, he settled at Salzburg. His mysticism is based upon natural science—chiefly in its chemical aspect—and upon the theosophy of the Kabbala. He continued to practise alchemy, and taught a mystical pantheism which not seldom degenerated into superstition. In his vain conceit he aimed at solving all mysteries, human and divine, and claimed to have found the philosopher's stone. Though the effect of his scholarly attainments was considerably neutralized by his overweening vanity, some of his philosophical tenets, such as for instance his distinction between faith and reason, have gained currency in more modern times. In his mystic philosophy, Valentine Weigel (1533–88), a greatly revered Lutheran preacher in Saxony, accepts the fantasies of Agrippa and Paracelsus, and rejects the scholasticism countenanced at the Reformation. Not daring openly to attack the prevailing orthodoxy, he privately elaborated his system, which remained unknown until after his decease, his writings appearing only in 1612. Although emphatically pantheistic, he does not minimize the importance of the human personality. On the contrary, and in sharp antagonism to evangelical teaching, he asserts that everything necessary to be known about God and the world may be reached through the study of man himself. Outward forms assumed by the Church he values not at all, and its doctrines he regards as merely an allegorical wrappage of eternal truth. It is to be noted that along with the theosophic element his theology is largely moulded by the *Theologia Germanica*, and partly coincides with that of Sebastian Frank (1500–45). Like Weigel, Frank first espoused and then actively opposed the cause of the Reformation, railing against the intolerance of theologians and defending the Anabaptists. He advocated absolute freedom in religion, and drifted into a dreamy, mystical pantheism. In his view the work of the historic Jesus is to awaken the consciousness of the ideal, and so of the divine element in us which makes us one in nature with God. The special revelation claimed by him is nothing but the imaginary reflex of his own introspection. The continued influence of Paracelsus, the *German Theology*, Schwenkfeld, and Frank, is distinctly traceable in the writings of Weigel, by whom again it was transmitted to Jacob Boehme.

We are now in a position to estimate the relation of mysticism to the Reformation. The preparatory work done by the Teutonic mystics of the fourteenth century is eloquently appraised by R. A. Vaughan as follows : " Truly, with them, Mysticism puts on her beautiful garments. See her standing, gazing heavenward, ' her rapt soul sitting in her eyes,' and about her what a troop of shining ones ! There is Charity, her cheek wet with tears for the dead Christ and pale with love for the living ; carrying, too, the oil and the wine—for Mysticism was the good Samaritan of the time, and succoured bleeding Poverty, when priest passed by and Levite ; there is Truth, withdrawing worship from the form and superstitious substitute, transferring it from priest and pageantry to the heart alone with God, and pressing on, past every channel, toward the Fount Himself ; there Humility, pointing to the embers of consumed good works, while she declares that man is nothing and that God is all ; and there, too, Patriotism, and awakening Liberty — for Mysticism appealed to the people in their native tongue ; fashioned the speech and nerved the arms of the German nation ; gave heart to the Fatherland (bewildered in a tempest of fiery curses) to withstand, in the name of Christ, the vicar of Christ ; led on the Teutonic lion of her popular fable to foil the plots of Italian Reynard ; and dared herself to set at nought the infuriate Infallibility." [1] The great defect of this mysticism was laid bare by Luther's appeal to the Bible. The isolated and variable witness of the individual was insufficient ; it needed to be supplemented by an authority which no single mystic could lay claim to. This was found in the sacred Scriptures—an outward standard as visible and more venerable than the externalism of the Roman Church itself, and one to which all alike could appeal. The preparatory service of the mystics, in conjunction with the clearer testimony of the Word concerning the redemptive work of Christ, furnished the twin factors required to effect a reformation. While, however, the German and Dutch mystics are rightly adjudged to be precursors of the Reformation, it must not

[1] *Hours with the Mystics*, Bk. viii. ch. i.

be supposed that they felt it incumbent upon them to assail the teaching of the Church as the Reformers did. Yet by their settled dislike of fixed mechanical formulas they naturally stressed the doctrines deemed vital to the inner life, and paid little or no heed to all else. Hence a treatise like the *Imitation* of Thomas à Kempis can be read to edification by Catholic and Protestant alike. Mysticism, moreover, from its exclusive cultivation of sheer inwardness, could set no bounds to the vagaries of individual piety. While its votaries revolted against the authority of the Church, that of the Scriptures was equally obnoxious to them. In reply to Luther's demand that he should justify his contentions by the teaching of Scripture, a certain Cellarius, a schoolmaster, declared it an insult " to speak so to a man of God." Clearly, as Luther discovered in connexion with the unreasonable extravagances of the notorious Thomas Münzer and afterwards of the Anabaptists, and with the lack of restraint shown in the Peasants' War, although mysticism could break up society into fragments, it could not build it up again on new foundations. If had no fixed standard of control, no iron waistband such as mere opposition to the external could never supply.

What, it may be asked, was the attitude in England towards Mysticism in pre-Reformation times ? The general opinion has been that it was unsympathetic, or at least one of indifference, if not of hostility. According to Dr. Inge, however, this is a mistaken view, and in support of his contention he adduces two examples of English mediæval mystics towards the close of the fourteenth century. One is Juliana of Norwich, who claimed to have in 1373 experienced certain " revelations " of a threefold character, namely, " by bodily sight, by words formed in the understanding, and by ghostly sight." Concerning the last-named category she says, " I cannot or may not shew it as openly or as fully as I would." The most assured of her visions were caused by a " divine illapse " into the mind, which occurred sometimes when she was asleep, but usually during waking hours. By quotations from these " revelations," Inge illustrates Juliana's devotion to the crucified Jesus, the value she attached to the means of grace, and her faith in the efficacy of inward prayer. Her assertion

that " in every soul that shall be saved there is a godly
will that never assented to sin," is, as the Bampton lecturer
points out, doubly interesting as an echo of the Neoplatonic view that the sins of the lower do not soil the
higher self, and as an equivalent of the " spark " of
Eckhart and other German mystics. A distinctly pantheistic strain is contained in the statement : " I saw no
difference between God and our substance, but, as it were,
all God. . . . God is God, and our substance a creature
in God. . . . Our soul is *made* Trinity, like to the unmade
Blessed Trinity, known and loved from without beginning,
and in the making oned to the Maker." Regarding the
existence of evil she says : " Often I wondered why the
beginning was not letted ; but Jesus, in this vision,
answered and said : " Sin is behovable (=necessary),
but all shall be well." Juliana had to be satisfied with
this assurance without knowing " *how* it shall be done."
This view of the " behovableness " of sin is not only
radically wrong in itself, but quite misrepresents the
attitude of Christian mysticism. It is even contrary to
her own teaching. In her *Revelation of Divine Love* she
writes : " If there were laid before me all the pain that
is in hell and purgatory and in earth . . . and sin, I had
liefer choose all that pain than sin. . . . To me was shewn
no harder hell than sin." On the other hand she never
tired of recording the words spoken to her by the Lord :
" I love thee, and thou lovest Me, and our love shall never
be disparted in two." These extracts from her book leave
the impression that though she was " honest " and " sane,"
she was also besides being imperfectly educated, somewhat too visionary. Still, apart from these aspects of her
personality, she certainly deserves to be ranked as a mystic,
albeit not of the highest type.

Dr. Inge's other example of an English mediæval mystic
is Walter Hilton (*ob.* 1396), a canon of the house of
Augustine at Thurgarten in Nottinghamshire. His chief,
though not his only, work is the *Ladder of Perfection*, which
has still many (mostly Roman Catholic) readers. The
extracts given by Inge show that Hilton regarded the
experience of the highest stage of contemplation, which
does not include visions and revelations, as both rare and
brief, but whenever it is enjoyed, " reason is turned into

light and will into love." In his judgement the prayer of quiet is prayer at its zenith—an estimate diametrically opposed to that of John Wesley, who was averse to silent prayer, and even condemned it as unscriptural—and extempore vocal prayer is relegated to the second degree of contemplation. Hilton lays stress on the crucified Jesus as the first object of the heart's affection. Owing to our inability to bear the pure light of the Godhead, " we must live under the shadow of His manhood as long as we are here below." Sin he reckons as a false love of self, and love of the world as a false light which plunges the soul into darkness—a darkness which, however, is only the har-binger of " the true day." By shutting out " distracting noises " we may hear Christ who sleeps within our heart." Plainly, Hilton was no believer in the " negative way."

E. Herman calls him " that most humble and sweet spoken of English mystics," pointing out that " he wrote for such as had not even a working acquaintance with everyday religious language." [1] In his writings there is certainly no suggestion of the esoteric spirit, or any claim that a mystic faculty is necessary in order to experience mystic vision. This claim, put forward by many of the older mystics, has been revived in a modified form by Miss E. Underhill.[2] So far from holding, as was formerly alleged, that mystic apprehension is the result of lulling to sleep the ordinary powers of the soul, she regards it as following upon their being awakened to new and united life. But she differentiates between the mystical faculty and the entire rational side of life connected with " feeling, thought, and will," and rates the one as superior to the other. She traverses the opinion of the Greek Fathers, who rightly considered that there is nothing abnormal in suscepti-bility to God. For man He is both the fountain and the goal of life. Although the spiritual instinct may be exceptionally keen in those usually termed mystics, it is essentially a natural impulse that leads human nature to cry out for the living God. This is not the exclusive privilege of an inner circle endowed with a psychological faculty denied to others. In some degree, surely, every true Christian is a mystic.

[1] *The Meaning and Value of Mysticism*, p. 36.
[2] *Mysticism*, p. 58 ff.

PART III

POST-REFORMATION MYSTICISM

AFTER the Reformation it was realized by the papal authorities that if the onward march of Protestantism was to be arrested, a revival of Catholic mysticism was indispensable. From this point of view the most hopeful field was Spain, a land at that time eminent for scholarship as well as notable for loyalty to the doctrine and discipline of the Roman Church. Wherever mysticism of an inferior type prevailed, or anything appeared in the visions of female saints corresponding to the " religious somnambulism " experienced in the Greek Church, the crushing hand of the Inquisition made itself felt. Nor did it fail sometimes to stretch itself out against even Teresa herself, who, however, escaped the imprisonment actually suffered by her disciple, St. Juan of the Cross. Their offence was not doctrinal, for they steadily conformed to the teaching of the Church, but in visionary experience and extreme asceticism they seemed to overpass the bounds of reason. Dr. Inge rightly remarks that " neither of them was a typical mystic, and that it was Teresa's confessor, Pedro of Alcantara, who was " the real founder of Spanish quietistic Mysticism." It was by reason of her zealous advocacy of a counter-reformation that Santa Teresa came prominently to the front. In the ardour of her practical labours the " Imaginary Visions " which bulked so largely in her earlier conventual life are stated by her to have ceased, " but," she adds, " the intellectual vision of the three Persons and of the Humanity seems always to be present."

A. *CATHOLIC*

I. SPANISH MYSTICS

(I) *Santa Teresa*

Born of noble lineage at Avila, a city of Old Castile, in 1515, Teresa Cepeda Davila y Ahumada took the veil while not yet nineteen, and was an inmate of the local Carmelite convent of the Encarnacion. One day, on entering the oratory, she was arrested by an image of the wounded Christ, and tearfully threw herself down before it, finally renouncing the world. Henceforth her life was not to be her own, but the life which, to use her own strong phrase, God lived in her. Teresa had now, at the age of forty-one, attained to the highest of the four degrees of prayer described in her autobiography, and frequently experienced a state of rapture or ecstatic trance which came upon her suddenly and irresistibly, and which was now full of sweetness, and anon full of pain. " Even sometimes when I was reading," she says, " there came suddenly upon me a sense of the presence of God, which did not allow me to doubt that He was within me, or that I was entirely engulfed in Him. This not after the manner of a vision : I believe it is called Mystic Theology ; it suspends the soul, which seems altogether beside herself." Apparently through the indiscretion of a priest in whom she confided, her unusual experiences were noised abroad, and she was voted a frenzied visionary. But, in 1557, Teresa had an interview with Francis Borgia, the principal saint of his Order, who declared that her visions were the work of God's Spirit, and that she should freely yield herself to His influence. Formerly she had divine " locutions " (such as *e.g.* " Have no fear, daughter, for it is I, and I will not desert thee," " Now, Teresa, be courageous," etc.) ; now she saw the Saviour ever close beside her—at first the crucified, and then the glorified Lord. About this time (1560) she had the vision of an angel who pierced her heart with a fire-tipped spear (known as the Transverberation). Interpreted by her devotees as the seal of sanctity, this became a favourite subject for representation in Spanish art. The psychology of all this she never professed to understand, but she prayed to be saved from delusions. Her vision was, of course, purely intellectual.

After years of self-contemplation in the cloister, Teresa was seized with a desire to go and " do something in the service of God." At this time devout Catholics were greatly exercised over the progress of the Reformation. Attributing the widespread defection to the lack of strict discipline within the religious communities, Teresa resolved to establish a " house " on the basis of the rigorous rules originally laid down for the Carmelite Order. Not without considerable opposition on the part of the Provincial of the Order, and of the sisters of the Encarnacion, who preferred to live under the " mitigated " rule, she succeeded in obtaining from Rome permission to found an unendowed monastery of the Carmelite Order of Descalzos or " Barefoots " (=sandalled) on the basis of poverty and a strictly ascetic life. Overjoyed at what had been accomplished, and in order to signalize her complete severance from the past, Teresa de Cepeda of Ahumada now began to call herself Teresa de Jesus, the sinner. At this juncture she was officially transferred from the Encarnacion to act as superintendent of the sisters at San José, where she remained for five restful years.[1]

The fifteen years that were still to be given her (1567–82) were years of incessant toil. Never brought into real contact with the Reformation of Luther and Melanchthon, and misconceiving its true character, Teresa viewed it as a deplorable defection from the Church, and ascribed it to the decay of strict discipline within the religious Orders. She therefore determined to set on foot a sort of counter-reformation, and to this (in her eyes) holy cause she devoted henceforth her first-rate ability, her ceaseless energy, and her buoyant faith. Her labours took the form chiefly of travel for the purpose of founding additional monasteries of discalced friars and nuns, permission to do this having been obtained from the General of her Order

---

[1] Excepting the quotations from her own writings, and the concluding paragraph, what follows here is abridged from my " Introduction " to Saint Teresa in the *Library of the Soul* series (T. C. & E. C. Jack).

(Father Rossi), whose sympathies were entirely with her.[1] After eight "houses" had been established, some of them not without serious difficulty, Teresa acted for three years as Prioress of the Encarnacion. Although her appointment to this post was distasteful alike to herself and to the nuns there, her gentle spirit soon disarmed all opposition, so much so that her departure called forth feelings of deep regret on the part of the sisterhood. Ultimately, in 1580, to her great joy, the Descalzos were granted leave, as an independent body, to choose their own provincial generals. Between 1562 and 1582 no fewer than fifteen monasteries for discalced friars, and seventeen for nuns, were founded by her personal efforts. Worn out by privation and fever, Teresa died peacefully at Alba, on the 4th October 1582, with these words of the Psalmist's upon her lips : " A broken and a contrite heart, O God, thou wilt not despise."

Of Teresa it may safely be said that she was one of the most remarkable women who have ever lived. Cherishing the loftiest ideals, she knew also how to handle practical affairs. Her mysticism was never divorced from good sense. She was born to rule. The monasteries she founded were standing proofs of her organizing power. Naturally shrewd, she quickly saw through the faults of her confessors. Being, however, without a spark of mean-ness, she did not canvass these before others, but gently hinted at them to the Fathers themselves. Courageous to a degree, she would lead the way in fording the floods, and would endure pain, misrepresentation, or persecution like a Stoic. She was also very loyal to friends, and dis-played great tenacity of purpose. Mrs. Cunninghame Graham describes her as " the noblest, most unselfish, most heroic, and the cleverest woman that Mediævalism ever produced." To all her womanly virtues and graces she even added some of the best features of a noble manli-ness. " A woman for angelical height of speculation," says Crashaw, " for masculine courage of performance more than a woman ; who, yet a child, outran maturity, and durst plot a martyrdom."

As a writer, Teresa is characterized by great charm of

---

[1] Full particulars may be gleaned from *The History of her Founda-tions*, written by herself, or from Mrs. Cunninghame Graham's exhaustive and able study.

style. What she has to say she says clearly, suitably, and concisely. Gleams of humour and irony relieve the solemnity of her pages. According to Froude, " the best satire of Cervantes is not more dainty." Her similes, taken mostly from nature and the simple life around the walls of her convent, are inimitably fine. A modern historian of Spanish literature says : " She ranks as a miracle of genius, as, perhaps, the greatest woman who ever handled pen, the single one of all her sex who stands beside the world's most perfect masters." [1] Even this tribute is excelled in Crashaw's deathless line :

> O 'tis not Spanish but 'tis Heaven she speaks.

In addition to her *Life*, the history of her *Foundations*, and her famous *Constitutions*, her works include sacred songs, numerous excellent *Letters*, abounding in " wit, vivacity, and playfulness," and various treatises of mystical religion, the principal of which are *The Way of Perfection* and *The Interior Castle*, or *Mansions of the Soul*.

Appended here are some extracts from her writings, which may serve not only as specimens of her compositions, but also as illustrations of the character of her mysticism.

(1) Regarding Visions she writes :

" Like imperfect sleep which, instead of giving more strength to the head, doth but leave it the more exhausted, the result of mere operations of the imagination is but to weaken the soul. Instead of nourishment and energy she reaps only lassitude and disgust : whereas a genuine heavenly vision yields to her a harvest of ineffable spiritual riches, and an admirable renewal of bodily strength " (*Life*, ch. xxviii.).

(2) On Contemplation :

" Whoever does not know how to place the men at chess, will not be able to play well : and if he know not how to give ' Check,' he will not know how to give ' Check-mate.' This is the mistake we all make, namely, that if any one accustom herself to think every day for a short time upon her sins (which every one ought to do if he be a practical Christian), people immediately call her a great

[1] J. Fitzmaurice Kelly, *Spanish Literature*, p. 193.

' Contemplative,' and would have her instantly possess as high virtues as he is bound to have who is eminent for Contemplation, and even she herself imagines so too, but she is mistaken.   She has not learnt at first how to arrange the men ; she thinks it is sufficient to know the pieces in order to ' checkmate,' but this is impossible, for the King will not give Himself up in the way we are speaking of, except to him who surrenders himself entirely into His hands " (*The Way of Perfection*).

(3) On Revelations mystically conveyed :

" One day, being in orison, it was granted me to perceive in one instant how all things are seen and contained in God.   I did not perceive them in their proper form, and nevertheless the view I had of them was of a sovereign clearness, and has remained vividly impressed upon my soul.   It is one of the most signal of all the graces which the Lord has granted me. . . . The view was so subtile and delicate that the understanding cannot grasp it. . . . Suppose the Godhead to be as some bright diamond, a vast globe of light, larger than the whole world, and that all our actions are seen in that all-embracing globe.   It was something like that I saw.   For I saw all my most filthy actions gathered up and reflected back upon me from that World of light.   It was an amazing and dreadful thing to see.   I knew not where to hide myself, for that shining light, in which was no darkness at all, held the whole world within it, and all worlds.   You will see that I could not flee from its presence.   Oh that they could be made to see this who commit deeds of darkness !   Oh that they but saw that there is no place secret from God.   Oh the madness of committing sin in the immediate presence of a Majesty so great, and to whose holiness all our sin is so hateful !   In this also I saw His great mercifulness in that he suffers such a sinner as I am still to live " (*Life*, ch. xxxvi.).

Teresa states that at another time, during her recitation of the Athanasian Creed, " Our Lord made me comprehend in what way it is that one God can be in three Persons. He made me see it so clearly that I remained as extremely surprised as I was comforted, . . . and now, when I think of the holy Trinity, or hear It spoken of, I understand how the three adorable Persons form only one God, and I experience an unspeakable happiness"(*Life*, ch. xxxv.).

In particular, she dwells fondly on the vision of our Lord's Humanity and its attendant spiritual blessings :

" My spirit was so absorbed that it seemed to be absolutely out of my body. . . . And then I saw the most sacred Humanity of our Lord in a more excessive glory than ever I had discerned before. Now this was represented to me by a certain admirable and clear notice of His being placed in the very bosom of His Father. . . . I saw myself present before that very Divinity. I remained so amazed that I think there passed some days before I was able to return to myself ; and still I conceived that I had that Majesty of the Son of God present with me, though not like the former. Howsoever it remaineth so engraven in my imagination that I cannot be rid of it for a little space, how short soever the time were wherein it was represented to one, and this is both a great comfort and also benefit to my soul. I have seen this Vision three other times ; and this, in my opinion, is the most sublime vision which ever our Lord shewed one ; and it brings the greatest benefits with it. For it seems that the soul is greatly purified by it, and that it doth utterly take away all strength from our sensuality. It is a vehement flame which seems to burn up, and even annihilate all the desires of this life. . . . And it is of great instruction for the raising up of our desires unto the pure truth. There remains a reverence of God imprinted after a certain manner which I know not how to describe ; but it is of a very different kind from whatsoever we can acquire here. It creates also a huge amazement in the soul to consider how she ever durst, or how any creature can presume so far as to offend such an exceeding great Majesty " (*Life*, ch. xxxiv.).

With this we may compare the statement in ch. xxviii. :

" If there were no other thing in Heaven to delight our sight but the excessive beauty of glorified bodies, that felicity would be immense ; especially to behold the Humanity of Jesus Christ our Lord, an exceeding great Glory. For since the Majesty thereof is discovered to be so great, whensoever it is represented to us here according to that proportion whereof our misery, in this mortal life of ours, is capable ; what will it be then, when we shall entirely enjoy so high a good ? "

(4) On the difference between Union and Rapt or Ecstasy :

" I would be glad to know how to declare the difference which is between Union on the one side, and Rapt and Flight of Spirit on the other ; for these two latter do signify in substance but one thing, and it is also called Ecstasy. The advantage is very great which belongs to Rapt, beyond Union ; and the effects also which it produces are much greater ; and it hath also many other operations. For mere union seems to be always after the same manner, both in the beginning, in the middle, and in the end ; and it is always in the interior part. But now, as Rapts are visitations of the soul in a higher strain, they are wont to produce their effects not only interiorly but exteriorly also. . . . In these Rapts it doth not seem that the soul doth even animate the body, and so the body itself remains with a kind of trouble and defect, through the want of the natural heat, and goes on cooling itself, though yet with an excessive sweetness and delight. . . . You find yourself to be carried away, and know not whither. . . . For here the soul must be content to hazard all, come on it what will, and to leave herself wholly in the hands of God, and to go whithersoever she shall be carried with a good will " (*Life*, ch. xx.).

(5) On the spiritually beneficial effects of the Ecstatic State :

" These effects are great. For first, the mighty power of our Lord is made apparent thereby ; and that, when his Divine Majesty is pleased to dispose of things otherwise, we are no more able to detain our bodies than our souls ; nor are we lords thereof, but must, though against our will, acknowledge that there is a Superior, and that these favours come from him, and that of ourselves we can do nothing in nothing ; and so a great impression of humility is made upon the soul by this means. And, further, I confess that it bred also a great fear in me to see that a massy body should be taken up from the earth. . . . There

4

doth also hereby appear so great a Majesty in him who
can do this, that it makes even the very hair of the head
stand on end, and there remains a mighty fear to offend
so great a God ; but yet so as that it is wrapped up in an
excessive kind of love which she conceives anew towards
him whom we find to carry so great a love to such rotten
worms as we are. . . . The soul well understands that
all this is none of her own, nor doth she know how she
comes to obtain so great a blessing, but she understands
clearly the exceeding great benefit and advantage which
every one of these Rapts brings to her. There is none
who can credit this but such an one as hath learned it by
experience. . . . The world is apt to conceive such endeavours are but impertinences and temptations ; yet,
if men would but understand that they are not things
which grow from herself, but from our Lord, to whom she
hath already delivered up the keys of her will, they would
not so much wonder at it. For my part I am of opinion
that a soul which comes once to this state doth already
neither say nor do anything of herself, but that this
Sovereign King takes care of all. . . . The soul is also
much afflicted with the thought of that time wherein she
took any care of points of honour, and for the gross error
wherein she was to believe that to be honour which the
world calls honour ; for she sees that it was an abominable
lie, and yet that everybody lives in the practice of it.
But now this soul understands that genuine honour is not
built upon a lie, but truth ; esteeming that to be worth
somewhat, which indeed is so ; and holding that which
indeed is nothing in no account at all ; since all is nothing,
and less than nothing, which perishes and pleaseth not God.
She laughs at herself that there should ever have been a
time when she made any care of money or desired it. . . .
Oh, if men would but agree to reckon it as so much useless
mud, what harmony would then reign in the world ! How
sincerely would all men perform acts of friendship if our
interest in honour or in money were extinct ! For my
part I conceive it would remedy all our ills " (*Life*,
ch. xx., and other kindred passages).

(6) On Learning and Intellect :

" I always had a great respect and affection for intel-

lectual and learned men. It is my experience that all
who intend to be true Christians will do well to treat with
men of mind and books about their souls. The more
learning our preachers and pastors have the better. For
if they have not much experience themselves, yet they
know the Scriptures and the recorded experiences of the
saints better than we do. The devil is exceedingly afraid
of learning, especially where it is accompanied with
humility and virtue. For my own part, I bless God continually, and we women, and all such as are not ourselves
intellectual or learned, are always to give God infinite
thanks that there are some men in the world who take
such great pains to attain to that knowledge which we
need but do not possess. And it delights me to see men
taking the immense trouble they do take to bring me so
much profit, and that without any trouble to me. I have
only to sit still and hear them. I have only to come and
ask them a question. Let us pray for our teachers, for
what would we do without them ? " (*Life*, ch. xiii.).

(7) The Prayer of Quiet :

" This is something supernatural, which we cannot
acquire by all our diligence, because it is settling the soul
in peace ; or rather, to speak more correctly, our Lord
leads her into peace by His presence, just as he did holy
Simeon, for all the faculties are calmed. The soul understands in a manner different from understanding by the
exterior senses, that she is now placed near her God, and
that in a very short time she will become one with Him
by union. This does not happen, because she sees Him
with the eyes of the body, or of the soul ; for as holy
Simeon saw this glorious little Infant only under the appearance of poverty, and wrapped in swaddling clothes, and
with attendants to follow Him, he might rather have
supposed He was the son of some mean person, than the
Son of the Heavenly Father. But the Child made Himself
known to him : and so in the same way the soul understands He is there, though not with the like clearness,
for she herself knows not how she understands, but that
she sees herself in the kingdom (at least near the King
who is to give it to her), and the soul seems impressed with

such reverence, that then she dare not ask anything"
(*The Way of Perfection*).

Teresa's writings, which were influenced by, and are in
some respects comparable to, the *Confessions* of Augustine,
contain the completest exposition not only of Spanish
Mysticism, but also of Catholic Mysticism generally.
Indeed there is probably no other instance of a woman
exercising such an influence upon any school of thought,
religious or other.   She is a shining figure in the annals of
Christian literature and piety.   Her status as a spiritual
force, not only in her own day but also since, is in keeping
with the strength and height of her spiritual aspirations.
Even before her canonization by Gregory XV. in 1622 she
had been voted by Parliament patron saint of Spain.   Her
elevation to this proud eminence was due no doubt to her
ascetic life, and to her mystic visions, of which she gives
an explanation in her *Interior Castle*.   But she has a
truer title to the name of saint than that conferred by a
place upon the Roman calendar : her life was hid with
Christ in God.   Her writings are perfumed with the
fragrance of an all-pervading humility.   They exhibit at
the same time a bright faith in the mercy of God through
Christ.   While seeking the good of others with a rare self-
forgetfulness, she had a single eye to the glory of God.
Her obedience was absolute, as was also the surrender of
her own will to the will of God.   There was nothing which
she would not do, nothing which she would not bear, in
the service of her Lord.   All lesser loves, including that of
self, were sunk in the ardent love of God.   Her so-called
autobiography shows us one who literally prayed without
ceasing.   Teresa, in short, was entirely devoted to God, a
heavenly-minded saint if ever there was one.   All who
are familiar with her writings will endorse the verdict of
Bishop Palafox : " I have not met with a single spiritual
man who does not become a passionate admirer of Santa
Teresa."

In his *Hours with the Mystics* (Book iii. chs. i. and ii.),
described by E. C. Gregory as "that unsatisfactory but
indispensable book," R. A. Vaughan strikes a strangely
discordant note in his estimate of Teresa.   " Her intellect
was never strong " ; she enjoined and practised " blind
obedience to ecclesiastical superiors " ; " wherever the

tears of Teresa fell, new seeds of superstition sprang up ; after her twentieth year she contracted " a strange complication of maladies—cramps, convulsions, catalepsis, vomitings, faintings, etc.," and some of the trances she subsequently experienced, and regarded as supernatural, " may have been bodily seizures of a similar kind " ; " she knew little of that charity which makes gracious inroads on the outer world " ; " her ascetic zeal was directed, not for, but against, the mitigation of suffering"; " she convulses herself with useless fervours, absolutely ignorant of all things and persons non-ecclesiastical." " Of the past career of Mystical Theology she is utterly ignorant." So unreservedly is she in the hands of her confessor that her soul depends wholly upon " the twist of the ecclesiastical thumb " ; for her, holy water is even more efficacious than the cross in overcoming the temptations of the devil ; the grossness of her secret visions of torments for the bad, of her investiture with a white garment of marvellous splendour, and of such heavenly objects as " Jesuits, sword in hand, with resplendent faces, gloriously hewing down heretics " ; " the confessions of Teresa are a continual refutation of her counsels " ;—while all this is strongly emphasized, her many excellences are virtually ignored. Some of the criticisms are no doubt well grounded, but Vaughan's whole attitude toward the saint is unsympathetic. Almost his only mitigating statement is that " such a life is an object of compassion more than blame. She was herself a victim of the wicked system to which her name was to impart a new impulse." If mistaken in some of her judgements and acts, she at any rate walked according to her light, and if she was biased against the Reformation, she was hardly more so than Vaughan seems to have been against her.

(2) *St. Juan of the Cross*

St. Juan of the Cross is a prominent name in Spanish Mysticism. As a zealous friar of St. Teresa's reform he established many houses of Carmelite contemplative and discalced nuns who lived under a rigorous rule, and in some cases even supplemented it by voluntary additions. St. Juan had nothing of the sunny personality and happy

humour that characterized his popular friend. As
practised by him, religion took on a hard and forbidding
aspect. He had an insatiable desire for suffering of the
most poignant and humiliating type, and if his conception
of holiness as the recompense of such self-immolation has
a certain moral grandeur about it, he cannot escape the
charge of fanaticism. His penances were so severe that
" he gave his body no rest." For him, in fact, religion
meant torture, and apparently he never realized the win-
someness and gentleness of Christ. He frequently fell into
trances, kept long vigils, and is said to have experienced
and to have wrought miracles. In an English biography [1]
are detailed many instances of St. Juan's hunger for
suffering, and of miracles said to have been either experienced or wrought by him.

As an example of the former may be mentioned a tale
told relating to a worldly nun in Avila whose conversion
he had brought about. " The poor nun returned to her
cell fully resolved to serve God only for the rest of her days,
and broke off from all her former levities. But one
of those who too often frequented the parlour of her
monastery, a wealthy and powerful personage in Avila,
was not pleased at her conversion. She never would see
him or any other idler as of old, and accordingly he resolved
upon revenge. He knew well enough whose influence had
been stronger than his, so he waited one night near the
monastery of the Incarnation, for the coming forth of
St. John of the Cross from the confessional of the church,
according to his wont. The saint came out and was going
towards his house when this man fell upon him, and beat
him so cruelly that he was nearly dead. Though he knew
who it was, and knew, too, why he was thus insulted, he
never complained, and never said who it was that had thus
been so merciless to him. But he did say afterwards to
some of his brethren that he never was so happy in all his
life as he was then, suffering for the sake of justice, and
that the blows of the angry man were as sweet to him as
the shower of stones to St. Stephen, the first martyr."

The following is a sample of the miraculous attributed
to St. Juan : " One day a violent tempest arose, the sky
was darkened, and the thunder roared ; the ground was

[1] *Life of St. John of the Cross*, by David Lewis, M.A. (1897).

burrowed by the rain of a raging hailstorm. The whole community was alarmed, but the saint was unmoved. He came down from his cell, and in the sight of the terrified fathers took off his cowl, and with it made the sign of the cross four times towards the four quarters of the heavens, and at once the clouds parted, and the sky was calm, and no sign of the storm remained."

Worn and wasted by his severe ascetic practices, and by cruel ill-treatment, Juan of Avila's strength gave way. In 1534 he was impeached before the Inquisition, and five years afterwards one of his books was condemned and placed upon the Index. In 1578 he was thrown into prison and kept in a narrow cell for more than eight months, and was never allowed to change his clothes. For all this the Friars of the Mitigation were responsible. They considered that they were acting within their powers, but apparently they had no real jurisdiction over him. Yet he who had prayed for sufferings uttered no word of protest. Later on, in 1591, he was harshly dealt with by the prior of Ubeda, and was involved in serious persecution, when deliverance came to him through sickness and death. He passed peacefully away in December of that year while not yet fifty. For five years he had lived under the primitive observance, and for twenty-three in the reform of St. Teresa, in whose eyes he was " a heavenly and divine person." He was canonized by Benedict XIII. in 1726.

St. Juan's principal writings are *The Ascent of Mt. Carmel* and *The Obscure Night*. They are characterized by an ardently devout spirit. His special standpoint as a mystic is revealed in a single sentence from the first of these works : " The journey of the soul to the Divine union is called *night* for three reasons : the point of departure is privation of all desire, and complete detachment from the world ; the road is by faith, which is like night to the intellect ; the goal, which is God, is incomprehensible while we are in this life." Like Dionysius, he plunges into " a darksome night " in which his natural powers of understanding, will, and memory become dead, and are replaced by higher and heavenly substitutes which function in no human manner, but as truly divine. The first night is that of the sense, in which the aspiring soul is introduced to supernatural delights hitherto unknown to the flesh.

The second night is that of the spirit, in which the soul, temporarily forsaken of God, seems to descend into the hell of utter midnight in order to the passive loss of the Nothing in the All. Thus only, denuded of natural knowledge and affection, can we attain to total darkness and the bliss of beholding the Infinite. The third night is that of the memory and the will, in which the soul experiences perfect oblivion, through which, however, these faculties are supernaturally transformed by the Divine Spirit and made to work divinely, with the result that all that should be remembered is remembered, and all lower enjoyments submerged in that of rest in God. In this supersensuous serenity the soul is immune from the machinations of the Devil.

Consequently, to shut out all created things, and shun the society of men ; to welcome the disagreeable, annihilate self, and in blind faith to renounce the guidance of reason, and at length in a state of passivity or unconscious trance, in which neither memory nor effort has any part, to reach the goal of the Infinite or union with God—such, according to St. Juan, is the path of the soul's ascent. To the quality of his mysticism even Vaughan pays tribute : It " takes the very highest ground. It looks almost with contempt upon the phantoms, the caresses, the theurgic toys of grosser mystics. In this respect, John is far beyond Teresa. He has a purpose ; he thinks he knows a way to it ; and he pursues it, unfaltering, to the issue. He gazes steadily on the grand impalpability of the Areopagite, and essays to mount thither with a holy ardour of which the old Greek gives no sign. And this, too, with the vision-craving sentimental Teresa at his side, and a coarsely sensuous Romanism all around him. . . . It is impossible not to recognize a certain grandeur in such a man. Miserably mistaken as he was, he is genuine throughout, as mystic and ascetic." [1] As in the case of Teresa, the *motif* underlying all his activity in thought and deed was the overthrow of Protestantism and the restoration of the Catholic practice of mediæval times. Both were leaders of the counter-reformation.

Although himself leading a life of continued mortification, San Juan strongly opposed the practice by certain

---

[1] *Op. cit.* ii. p. 194.

communities of friars and nuns of various irregularities and novelties with a view to a more rigorous life than that imposed by the rule and constitutions. Against this tendency to observe excessive penances and to strike out for themselves new ways of perfection, he delivers his judgement in *The Dark Night* (i. ch. vi.) as follows:

" Many beginners, delighting in the sweetness and joy which they find in such practices, seek after spiritual sweetness more than pure and true devotion, which is that which God regards and accepts in the whole course of the spiritual road. For which reason, over and above their imperfection in seeking after sweetness in devotion, the spirit of gluttony which has taken possession of them forces them to overstep the bounds of moderation, within which virtue is acquired and consists. Allured by the sweetness they find therein, some of them kill themselves by penance, and others weaken themselves by fasting, taking upon themselves, without rule or advice, more than their weakness can bear; they try rather to hide their doings from those whom they are bound to obey in the matter, and some even dare to practise austerities expressly forbidden them. These are full of imperfections, people without reason, who put aside discretion and submission and obedience which is the penance of reason, and therefore a sacrifice more sweet and acceptable to God than all the other acts of bodily penance. Bodily penance is full of imperfections, if that of the rule be neglected, because men are drawn to it simply because they like it, and find pleasure in it."

St. Juan's persistent object, however, was to set himself free from the yoke of the senses. In his view " the radical remedy lies in the mortification of the four great natural passions—joy, hope, fear, and grief. You must seek to deprive these of every satisfaction, and leave them comfortless and leave them as it were in darkness and the void. Let your soul therefore turn always not to what is most easy, but to what is hardest; not to what most pleases, but to what disgusts; not to desire the more, but the less; not to will anything, but to will nothing; not to seek the best in everything, but to seek the worst, so that you may enter for the love of Christ into a complete destitution, a perfect poverty of spirit, and an absolute renunciation of everything in this world. To know all things, learn to know nothing. To possess all things, resolve to possess nothing. To get to where you have no taste for anything, go through whatever experiences you have no taste for. To come to the All you must give up the All. And if you should attain to owning the All, you must own it, desiring Nothing. In this spoliation the soul finds its tranquillity and rest." (Abridged from *Saint Jean de la Croix*, *Vie et Oeuvres*, ii. 94, 99.)

Regarding the intuitions by which the soul is divinely helped, the saint writes :

" They enrich it marvellously. A single one of them may be sufficient to abolish at a stroke certain imperfections of which the soul during its whole life had vainly tried to rid itself, and to leave it adorned with virtues and loaded with supernatural gifts. A single one of these intoxicating consolations may reward it for all the labours undergone in its life—even were they numberless. Invested with an invincible courage, filled with an impassioned desire to suffer for its God, the soul then is seized with a strange torment—that of not being allowed to suffer enough " (*ibid*. ii. 390).

St. Juan emphatically asserts that the highest state of mystical consciousness defies description, and that any attempt to elucidate it by means of sensible imagery is both futile and improper. In the mystical knowledge of God, " since the senses and the imagination are not employed, we get neither form nor impression, nor can we give any account or furnish any likeness, although the mysterious and sweet-tasting wisdom comes home so clearly to the inmost parts of our soul. Fancy a man seeing a certain kind of thing for the first time in his life. He can understand it, use and enjoy it, but he cannot apply a name to it, nor communicate any idea of it, even though all the while it be a mere thing of sense. How much greater will be his powerlessness when it goes beyond the senses ! This is the peculiarity of the divine language. The more infused, intimate, spiritual, and supersensible it is, the more does it exceed the senses, both inner and outer, and impose silence upon them. . . . The soul then feels as if placed in a vast and profound solitude, to which no created thing has access, in an immense and boundless desert, desert the more delicious the more solitary it is. There, in this abyss of wisdom, the soul grows by what it drinks in from the well-springs of the comprehension of love, . . . and recognizes, however sublime and learned may be the terms we employ, how utterly vile, insignificant, and improper they are, when we seek to discourse of divine things by their means" (*The Dark Night of the Soul*, ii. ch. xvii.).

(3) *Molinos*

An important name in the history of Spanish Mysticism is that of Miguel Molinos. He was born in December 1627 near Saragossa in Aragon. The scion of a noble family, he was educated at Coimbra, where he graduated in divinity, and for a number of years exercised the priestly office. Thereafter he migrated to Rome as the likeliest centre for the propagation of the mystical views which he had been led to entertain. Impressed with his learning and piety, Pope Innocent XI. conferred upon him many honours, and even housed him within the palace. In 1675 his notable book, *The Spiritual Guide*, was published in Italian, and when afterwards translated into Spanish, so great was its popularity in the land of his birth, as to engender the belief, still more or less prevalent, that the Spanish version was the original. In this treatise he ministered to the needs of earnest souls who longed to escape from the din of war and controversy, and taught them to look *within* for the peace denied them without. Although this point of view did not essentially differ from that of Tauler or Teresa, his glowing piety and saintly life appealed to multitudes who were weary of the fierce antagonisms of the current religion, like a fresh revelation worthy of being appropriated and put into practice. The success of his book was phenomenal. His real significance lies in the fact that by its publication he initiated a marked revival of spiritual religion throughout the Roman Catholic world of his day. In numerous localities of various lands, praying societies were formed, and with these he kept in touch by written correspondence. His method was properly enough called " New," for it meant paying little

heed to the religious machinery of external images and
acts, and of extreme asceticism, which was paralysing the
inner life of the spirit.   It was a call to be still, to wait
upon God in simplicity, in silence, and in faith, leaving
Him to act upon the soul and guide it into the way of
truth.   In his plea for the mystical as opposed to the
mechanical in devotional writings, he met with influential
support in Rome itself, while in Naples tens of thousands
heartily embraced his views.

As the advocate of a mystical theology, however, Molinos
aroused the hostility of the powerful Order of the Jesuits.
They felt that their craft was in danger, as indeed it was,
for if men can hold direct communion with God in the
silence of their own souls there is no necessity for the intervention of the priest.   The Confessional, too—that so
fruitful source of revenue—was threatened with extinction
if forgiveness could be sought and obtained at home.
Were this new movement to prevail, not only would the
coffers of the Church be depleted, and her whole administra-
tion left without the means of support, but a blow would
be struck at the hitherto persistent policy of bringing
influence to bear upon kings and rulers through their
priestly directors.   The Jesuits were shrewd enough to
perceive that unless the movement sponsored by Molinos
could be suppressed, the great and carefully constructed
external organization of the Church would be faced with
diplomatic as well as financial ruin.   Hence their determination to destroy it.

To Father Segneri, a famous and fanatical preacher of
their Order, was assigned the difficult task of opening the
campaign.   As Teresa and Catherine of Siena had both
been canonized, and as the " tenderness " of St. Francis
de Sales had also been utilized as a foil for Jesuitical
severity, Father Segneri could not make a frontal attack
upon Quietism.[1]   What he assailed was not the method
itself—indeed he praised it as likely to be helpful to ex-
ceptional saints—but only its unsuitability for the life of
the average Christian in the workaday world.   On the
publication of Segneri's discourse, however, less favour was
shown to him than to Molinos in high quarters at Rome,

---

[1] This term seems to have been first applied in connexion with
Molinos.

and when the Inquisition was called in to adjudicate, Segneri was condemned and his book put under the ban. So the Jesuits had to adopt another plan. They frequently acted as confessors and directors of princes, and in this way gained great influence over the French king Louis XIV, who, in return for offers of licence to play fast and loose with the Ten Commandments, was cunningly persuaded by his confessor to press for the denunciation of Molinos and all his works. By the powerful intervention of this monarch Molinos came under the relentless cruelty of the Inquisition, was betrayed at the royal behest by his quondam friend Cardinal d'Estrées, and was thrown into prison, where, probably in deference to the known partiality of the Pope, he was left to languish and suffer tortures for nearly two years before his so-called " trial " in 1687. This was brutally unfair, and a travesty of justice. Though ostensibly based upon an array of sixty-eight propositions, the accusation brought against Molinos was not that he had taught heretical doctrine ; its gravamen was that he and his adherents were leading impure lives— an infamous reversal of the truth. The real grievance of the Jesuits was that Molinos and his followers stood for strict purity of life, claimed independence of priestcraft in their approaches to God, neglected the Confessional, and deprecated the superstitions connected with image worship, veneration of relics, processions, and such-like observances. The farce ended, Molinos was condemned as a propagator of Quietism.

Why, it may be asked, should Molinos have been so summarily dealt with, while Teresa, Juan of the Cross, and Francis de Sales, whose teaching concerning the religion of the heart did not differ essentially from his, were not only tolerated, but in due course even canonized ? The reason is not far to seek. Although they shared his Quietistic views, and represented the nescience of ecstasy as never attained by an effort of the human will, but as divinely wrought, they nevertheless lent their support to the sensuous externalism of the Church, and the cultivation of the ceremonialism connected with images, crucifixes, pictures of the saints, and the lucrative practice of the Confessional. The charge brought against Molinos of reducing redemption to the sinking of self in the abstract

Godhead might as well have been made against Tauler and other pre-Reformation German mystics who used language similar to his without ever intending to ignore the humanity of Christ. What Molinos says is simply this : " Although the humanity of Christ is the most perfect and most holy mean of access to God, the highest mean of our salvation, yea, the channel through which alone we receive every blessing for which we hope, yet is the humanity not the supreme good, for that consists in the contemplation of God. But as Jesus Christ is what He is more through His Divine nature than His human, so that man contemplates Christ continually and thinks of Him, who thinks on God, and hath regard constantly to Him. And this is the case more especially with the contemplative man, who possesses a faith more purified, clear, and experimental." It was not so much on any point of doctrine, then, that Molinos was condemned, as on account of his disparagement of the artificial and mechanical methods of devotion sponsored by the mediæval Church. This was the head and front of his offending. Though he is said to have " saved his life by recanting," he was again committed to prison under a life sentence, and died in the dungeons of the Inquisition at Rome in December 1696. Severe measures were taken against his disciples, of whom no fewer than two hundred were put under arrest. In France, Bossuet brought about the imprisonment of Madame Guyon as the leading figure in Quietistic circles there. An end in short was put to a movement which, but for the malignant opposition of the Jesuits, might have liberated the Roman Catholic countries from the thraldom of an external, priest-ridden, and superstitious faith, and led them into the glorious liberty of the children of God.

As special points in the teaching of Molinos may be noted :

(1) The stress laid upon " internal recollection," by which is meant the pure act of faith and silence in the presence of God. In his judgement it concerns us only to prepare the heart like clean paper on which the Divine wisdom may make His own imprint. " Be not afflicted nor discouraged," he says, " to see thyself faint-hearted ; He returns to quiet thee, that still he may stir thee ; because this Divine Lord will be alone with thee, to rest

in thy soul, and form therein a rich throne of peace ; that within thine own heart, by means of internal recollection, and with His heavenly grace, thou mayest look for silence in tumult, solitude in company, light in darkness, forgetfulness in pressures, vigour in despondency, courage in fear, resistance in temptation, and quiet in tribulation." Again he says : " There are two ways that lead to the knowledge of God, the one remote, the other near ; the first is called speculation, the second, contemplation." The external way of seeking God is by meditation and rigorous penance. It is the way of beginners, but years of this external exercise leave them void of God and full of themselves. The truly spiritual pursue the interior way which leads to union with God through perfect resignation to His will and absolute passivity of soul, until it be filled with a supernatural infusion of the mystical grace. We enter into internal recollection through the humanity of our Lord Jesus Christ, first by meditating on the mysteries and on the Saviour's life and death, and then by contemplation or " eyeing " His Humanity and Passion in pure faith. Meditation prepares the way to contemplation, which is both active and passive, the latter being the higher stage. The means whereby the soul ascends to the felicity of contemplation are two : the pleasure and the desire of it. Molinos distinguishes three steps of infused contemplation—*satiety*, when the soul is filled with God, then it is quiet and satisfied with Divine love ; *intoxication*, an elevation of soul arising from Divine love ; and *security*, which casts out fear. He enumerates six other steps of contemplation—Fire, Union, Elevation, Illumination, Pleasure, and Repose—by which the soul rises higher, and adds a list of signs by which we may know the inner man and the mind that is purged. In thus departing from the general view that in the soul's ascent to perfection there are three stages—purgative, illuminative, and contemplative—and in virtually claiming that there is only one way, namely, the interior, Molinos was not an orthodox mystic, and this dictum was formally condemned by Innocent XI., notwithstanding his friendly esteem for the author of *The Spiritual Guide*.

(2) The value attached to the prayer of silence : " The Lord will have thee to walk by faith in silence." Quoting

Gerson to this effect : " Though I have spent forty years
in reading and prayer, yet I never find anything more
efficacious nor compendious for attaining to the mystical
theology than that our spirit should become like a young
child and beggar in the presence of God," he adds : " Walk
as if thou wert blindfolded, without thinking or reasoning ;
put thyself into His kind and paternal hands, resolving to
do nothing but what His Divine Will and Pleasure is."
According to Molinos, there are " three kinds of silence :
the first is of words, the second of desires, and the third
of thoughts. . . . By not speaking, nor desiring, and not
thinking, one arrives at the true and perfect mystical
silence, wherein God speaks with the soul, and in the
abyss of its own depths teaches it the most perfect and
exalted wisdom. . . . Thou art to keep thyself in this
mystical silence if thou wouldest hear the sweet and
Divine voice. . . . The perfection consists not in speaking
nor in thinking much on God, but in loving Him sufficiently,"
and this love is reached through " perfect resignation and
internal silence. . . . Mary Magdalene said not a word,
and yet the Lord Himself . . . became her panegyrist,
saying that she had loved much." To procure the
supreme internal peace " the Jonah of sense " must be
cast into the sea. The prayer of silence is " the highest
pitch of prayer " ; it is also " the easiest " and " the most
secure."

(3) The estimate put upon visions, confession, and outward religious observances. As regards visions, Molinos,
like St. Juan of the Cross, bluntly declares them to be not
seldom of Satanic origin. Unless for beginners, he is no
advocate for frequent confession. On the other hand, he
strongly insists upon careful attention to outward ordinances and, in particular, " daily communion, when possible."
At the same time he sharply discriminates between edifying
and unspiritual discourses. " The sermons of men of
learning, who lack the Spirit, though they are made up of
divers narratives, descriptions, acute discourses, and
exquisite proofs, yet are by no means the Word of God,
but the words of men. . . . Those that preach the word of
God with the Spirit make it take impression in the heart ;
but those that preach it without the Spirit carry it no
farther than to the ear."

The following is a further extract from *The Spiritual Guide* :

" It is the saying of St. Bernard that to serve God is nothing else but to do good and suffer evil. He that would go to perfection by the means of sweetness and consolation is mistaken ; you must desire no other consolation from God than to end your life for His sake in the state of true obedience and subjection. Christ our Lord's way was not that of sweetness and softness, nor did He invite us to any such, either by his words or example, when He said : ' He that will come after Me, let him deny himself, and let him take up his cross and follow Me.' The soul that would be united to Christ must be conformable to Him, and follow Him in the way of suffering. . . . O what a great happiness is it for a soul to be subdued and subject ! what great riches is it to be poor ! what a mighty honour to be despised ! what a height is it to be beaten down ! What a comfort is it to be afflicted ! what a credit of knowledge is it to be reputed ignorant ! and finally, what a happiness of happinesses is it to be crucified with Christ ! This is that lot which the Apostle gloried in—' God forbid that I should glory save in the cross of our Lord Jesus Christ.' Let others boast in their riches, dignities, delights, and honours : but to us there is no higher honour than to be denied, despised, and crucified with Christ. . . . To deny one's self in all things, to be subject to another's judgement, to mortify continually all inward passions, to annihilate one's self in all respects, to follow always that which is contrary to one's own will, appetite, and judgement, are things that few can do ; many are those that teach them, but few are they that practise them."

2. FRENCH MYSTICS

(1) *François de Sales (and Jeanne de Chantal)*

Born in 1567 at Annecy in France, Francis de Sales was at an early age appointed to the provostship of the Cathedral Church of Geneva, with a special commission to root out " heresy " from the regions of Chablais, Galliard, and Ternier. He set about this task with such

5

zeal that in less than two or three years he " extirpated
almost " the deep-seated attachment to the principles of
the Reformation which had distinguished those areas for
seventy years.   Afterwards consecrated Bishop of Geneva,
he became the most outstanding sacred orator of his time.
By his persuasive preaching at Paris in 1602 several
Huguenot nobles were induced to adhere to the orthodox
Catholic faith.   In order to retain him in France, King
Henry IV. offered him a better bishopric than that of
Geneva, but this he declined out of loyalty to his " first
spouse."   Reckoned a consummate theologian, he made
pronouncements regarding papal rights which prepared
the way for the later *Fathers of the Vatican*.   As a pillar
of the Church he worthily filled the gap between St.
Bernard and Bossuet, and it is significant that he was
revered alike by Bossuet, Fénelon, and St. Vincent de Paul.
Even Richelieu desired to negotiate with him.   In point of
character he was proverbially gentle, yet could be leonine
too, and in the latter respect his words can compare with
Anselm's imperious declaration :   " God loves nothing so
much as the liberty of His Church."   As the author of the
Introduction to the Devout Life, his fame spread throughout
the whole of Christendom, and even to-day he ranks high
in the domain of devotional literature.   Six years before
his death at Lyons, in December 1622, appeared his treatise
on *The Love of God*, which in respect of its revelation of
mystical ecstatic raptures greatly exceeds the former
treatise.

The Hebrew prophet's call to lovers of righteousness :
" Look unto Abraham your father and to Sarah your
mother " (Is 51^2), took on a fitting and more modern form
by the substitution for Abraham and Sarah of the names of
François de Sales and Jeanne de Chantal, " this patriarch
of the new law, and this widow, this Sarah, when they met
for the first time at Dijon in the year 1604." [1]   The widow
had been a child of genius, who (so it is said) at the age of
five victoriously routed a Calvinist in a dispute about the
Eucharist !   What is more certain is that after being
educated at a notable seminary she became an exemplary
wife and mother, and devoted her early widowhood to the

[1] Mgr. Touchet : *Saint François de Sales et Sainte Chantel :* Leur
Sanctification et leur Œuvre Communes.   Paris, 1911.

careful upbringing of her children. Distinguished for her charity, she was known among the poor as " the good lady."

When Madame de Chantal and Francis de Sales providentially met, both saints in virtue of their aptitude for spiritual realities were revealed to each other, and between them there was formed a peculiar bond of mutual confidence and esteem. The Bishop of Geneva kept his disciple informed about his work, confiding to her not only his cares, but also his literary aims and hopes. More especially he kept her in touch with his labours in the preparation of " our dear book " (*The Treatise of the Love of God*). On her part, Jeanne de Chantal steadily encouraged him in the prosecution of this work. With rare loyalty to him as a master, she considered his counsels as nothing short of laws prompted by the Holy Spirit. The bond between these two holy souls was of the most intimate nature. It was an " incomparable friendship " in which, while the flesh had no part, the secrets of conscience were candidly unveiled, and aspirations after perfection freely canvassed. To call it Platonic is not enough ; it was distinctly sanctifying. The bishop dealt rigorously with his daughter. In the early days of their acquaintance, on seeing her at the table of President Fermiot wearing some simple ornaments, he said to her, " Do you intend to marry again ? " She replied in the negative. " Then," said he, " put away the sign." She understood and discarded them. Her sensibility, however, quickly finds expression : " My father, my unique father, and everything that you are to me." Their close and ardent union is likewise reflected in the words of St. Francis : " I love this love incomparably." The spectacle of the virtues of the disciple helped him to aspire to still greater things for himself, and to urge upon her ever more absolute devotion in regard to taking up her cross. " You wish then, daughter, truly to serve Jesus Christ ? " " Truly." " Then you dedicate yourself wholly to His love ? " " Altogether, in order that He may transform me into Himself." " Do you consecrate yourself without reserve ? " " Yes, without reserve." " In fine, my daughter, you desire, then, God alone ? " " Nothing but Him for time and eternity." As for Francis, he said, " I am going to put my hand to our book concerning the love of God, and

I shall try to write as much of it on my heart as I shall put upon paper." Here we are verily on Alpine heights. "The two holy souls," says Mgr. Touchet, Bishop of Orléans, " appeared more admirable, alike to the angels, to man, and to God." [1] Their intimacy waxed stronger and stronger till the day of the mystical rupture dawned. He is aware the woman loves him with all her heart, but gently prepares the blow which he believes it to be his duty to strike. Intuitively she perceives the intention, and spares him the vexation of uttering the fatal word. He falls ill. She writes : " I am glad that you will preserve your solitude, because it will be employed in the service of your dear spirit. I have not been able to say ' our,' since it seems to me that I have no more a part in it, so much that I find myself denuded and stripped of all that was most precious to me." Although she bravely faced the situation, it is clear that she suffers in her innermost being. " Alas ! my unique father," she writes, " to-day there comes to me the remembrance that once you commanded me to despoil myself. I answered, ' I know not of what,' and you said to me, ' Have I not told you, my daughter, that I would strip you of all ? ' O God, how easy it is to quit what is around us ! But to quit one's skin, one's flesh, one's bone, and penetrate into the very marrow, as it seems to me we have done, that is a thing great, difficult, and impossible, except for the grace of God." It was the cry of a wounded dove.

In a book of captivating interest the Abbé Henri Brémond traverses the traditional view of the transformation by the gentle Bishop of Geneva of the rude and imperious Bourgignonne. As a result of his researches among old documents, he presents a portrait of the Baroness Chantal in which the saint loses nothing, but the woman gains much. Although in the friendly collaboration between the two saints there was nothing of a carnal nature, the tenderness of a woman's heart was not suppressed. This writer in fact protests against the sale of de Chantal to St. Francis de Sales. They are different, he states, but as a courageous woman without affectation she was not inferior to him. Madame de Chantal had shown her devotion to the virtues of the Spirit by refusing re-marriage when pressed thereto,

[1] *Op. cit.* p. 11.

and as for Francis de Sales, he was, as we have seen, stimulated to mount higher and higher by the sight of her virtues.   It was the natural consequence of their almost angelic life that, in 1610, they should have become the founders of an Order—that of the Nuns of *The Visitation*, of which Madame de Chantal became the first superior— a position for which she was exceptionally qualified as a mother, a succourer of the poor, and a *grande dame* who could keep her place with dignity as being first and last a disciple of Jesus.   Realizing the value of the instrument put into his hands, Francis de Sales resolved to embark upon the enterprise.   Most faithfully his fellow-labourer performed her part in visiting and caring both in things material and in things spiritual for the poor, the sick, and the afflicted.   The contemplation of Mary thus joined to the works of Martha wrought a revolution in the conception of a religious life, not only in France but beyond it.   After a few years, under the fostering care of Vincent de Paul and Mlle Legras, charitable institutions which were not monastic began to cover the world, and God blessed them.   Their houses were not " gardens enclosed," but centres of active Christian benevolence.   For M. Brémond, not the Bishop of Geneva, but Madame de Chantal, was the real founder of *The Visitation*, by teaching him many things not obvious to himself.   She set herself to be the living embodiment of the ideas which he developed before her.   It is in short the judgement of this writer that, if to-day the undisputed teacher of mysticism, he owes it under God to her who offered upon the Divine altar the sacrifice of her love, and taught the world that mysticism is not incompatible with patriotism.

St. Francis de Sale's attitude to mysticism cannot be said to have been altogether consistent.   As Dr. Inge remarks : " The somewhat feminine temper of Francis leads him to attach more value to fanciful symbolism than would have been approved by St. Juan or even by St. Teresa."   Still it must be recognized that, by toning down the rigours of Spanish Mysticism and presenting it in the flexible if somewhat feminine garb of an attractive pietism, he gave inspiration to many in search of lofty ideals of life. Although leaning towards Quietism, and even credited with attaining to ecstasy oftener than once, he sometimes

shows an opposite tendency, as for example when he
writes : " There are certain things by many esteemed
virtues which in truth are none at all. . . . I mean
ecstasies, raptures, insensibilities, impassibilities, deified
unions, revelations, transformations, and such-like perfec-
tions." [1] It may also be noted that in one of his frequent
references to the Virgin, Mary, de Sales makes a curious
departure from his usual sanity. The cult of Mariolatry
has certainly not diminished since his time, but few perhaps
have ever perpetrated so ridiculous an utterance as this :
" Honour, reverence, and respect with a special love the
sacred and glorious Virgin Mary. She is the mother of
our Sovereign Father, and consequently our Grand-
mother ! " [2] It is only fair to say that most of his references to " our Lady " are more discreet and in better taste,
and that upon the whole a more winsome devotional writer
can scarcely be conceived.

Appended are some brief extracts from *An Introduction
to a Devout Life* :

" Devotion is the pleasure of pleasures, the queen of
virtues, and the perfection of charity. If charity be milk,
devotion is the cream : if charity be a plant, devotion is
its flower : if charity be a precious stone, devotion is its
lustre : if charity be a rich balm, devotion is its odour,
yea the odour of sweetness, which comforts men, and
rejoices angels."

" The angels upon Jacob's Ladder have wings, yet they
fly not, but ascend and descend in order from step to step.
The soul, which rises from sin to devotion, is compared to
the dawning of the morning, which rising drives not away
the darkness in an instant, but by degrees."

" O world, O abominable troop ! no, never more shall you
see me under your banner. I have for ever left off your
fooleries and vanities. O king of pride, O cursed king,
infernal spirit, I renounce thee with all thy vain pomps,
I detest thee with all thy works. And turning myself to
Thee, my dear Jesus, King of felicity and immortal glory,
I embrace Thee with all the powers of my soul, I adore

[1] *The Devout Life*, pt. iii. ch. ii. 5.
[2] *Ibid.* pt. ii. ch. xvi. 3.

Thee with all my heart, I choose Thee now and ever for my King, and by my inviolable fidelity I pay Thee irrevocable homage, and submit myself to the obedience of Thy holy laws and ordinances."

" As the daylight increases, we see more clearly in the glass the spots and blemishes of our faces : even so as the inward light of the Holy Ghost more and more illuminates our consciences, we see more plainly and distinctly the sins, the inclinations, and imperfections which hinder us from attaining to true devotion ; and the selfsame light which causes us to discover those spots and deformities enflames us likewise with desire to cleanse and purge us from them."

" Gaming, masking, feasting, gallantry, comedies are no way hurtful, but indifferent, and may be used both well and ill ; yet notwithstanding these things are dangerous, and to bear an affection to them is yet more dangerous. . . . It is no sin to do such things, but it is sin to affect them."

" I recommend to you mental and cordial prayer, and especially that which has for its subject the life and passion of our Lord ; for beholding Him often by meditation, your soul will be filled with Him, you will learn His carriage, and frame your actions according to the model of His."

" Holy Elzear, Count of Arrian in Provence, having been long absent from his devout and chaste Delphina, she sent expressly a messenger to him, to inform herself of his health, and he made her this answer, ' I am very well, my dear wife ; but if you desire to see me, seek me in the wound of my blessed Saviour's side, for there I dwell, and there you shall find me, otherwise you will search for me in vain.' This was a right Christian cavalier indeed."

" Nobility of blood, favour of great persons, popular honour, these are things which are not in us, but either in our progenitors, or in the estimation of other men. Some there are that become proud and insolent by being upon a good horse, or for having a feather in their hat, or by wearing good clothes ; but who sees not their folly ? For if there be any glory in this, it belongs to the horse, the bird, and the tailor."

" There is a great difference between having poison and being poisoned. All apothecaries almost have poison to use upon diverse occasions, but yet they are not poisoned, because they have not poison in their bodies but in their shops : so you may have riches without being poisoned with them, if you keep them in your purse, or in your house, and not in your heart."

" They who treat of husbandry and country affairs tell us that if one write any word upon a very sound almond, and put it again into the shell, shutting it up very close, and so planting it, all the fruit which that tree produces will have the same word written and engraven upon it. For my part, I could never approve of their order and method who, to reform a man, begin with the exterior, as their gestures, apparel, and hair. On the contrary, I think it better to begin with the interior. ' Be converted unto Me,' saith God, ' with all your heart.' For the heart being the fountain of all our actions, they must needs be such as is the heart."

(2) *Madame Guyon (and Fénelon)*

Madame Guyon, *née* Jeanne Marie Bouvières de la Mothe, was born in 1648 at Montargis, some fifty miles to the south of Paris. Her parents were people of rank and influence, and were noted for their piety. About her twelfth year, the perusal of the writings of St. Francis de Sales, and the example of his disciple Madame de Chantal, led her earnestly to seek the gift of prayer. In order to imitate the latter as closely as possible, she wore upon her person, stitched on to her clothes, the sacred name of Jesus. Aiming at the most perfect life, she also practised the severest penances. In 1663, owing to a change of the family residence, Mademoiselle de la Mothe found herself suddenly thrown into the gaiety of Paris—never more pronounced than in the reign of Louis XIV. Endowed as she was with the combined charms of youth, beauty, and intellect, her " vanity increased." Offers of wedlock poured in upon her, and in 1664 she signed the articles of marriage, without knowing their purport, between herself and M. Guyon, a wealthy suitor of more than twice her own age. Her married life was far from happy. Her husband shewed her real affection, but weakly allowed himself to be swayed by his jealous and overbearing mother. On her side there was no pretence of having married for love ; till two or three days before she was led to the altar she had never seen her husband. In her distress Madame Guyon turned to God as the sole refuge left to her. She was gradually approaching a crisis in her spiritual history. The birth of a son ; pecuniary losses ; a serious illness ; the death of her favourite half-sister, and afterwards that of her mother ; the study of devotional works like the *Imitation of Jesus Christ* by Thomas à Kempis and the writings of Francis de Sales ; conversation with an exiled lady of singular piety, temporarily domiciled in her father's house, and with her cousin M. de Toissi, a missionary to the Chinese—all these things had an important bearing upon the inner transformation which she was about to experience. But the finishing touch was supplied by the remark of a holy Franciscan monk who chanced to visit her father. Having told him her difficulties about prayer, she got the answer : " It is, Madame, because you seek outside what you have within. Accustom yourself to seek God in your heart, and you will find Him there." Like an arrow, the words pierced her heart. To use her own expression, it was " quite changed." From the hand of Divine grace she had received in a moment what all her efforts had not availed to secure. " I was given an experience of God's presence in my central depth, not through thought or application of the mind, but as a thing one possesses really after the sweetest manner. . . . I experienced in my soul an unction which, like a soothing balm, healed all my wounds. . . . Nothing of my prayer passed into my head, but it was a prayer of enjoyment and possession in the will, where the delight of God was so great, so pure, and so simple, that it attracted and absorbed the other powers of the soul in profound concentration, without act or speech." In these significant words she already gives expression to the essential elements of the Quietism with which her name has become permanently associated.

From henceforth she steadfastly aimed at what she calls " annihilation of the powers " through absorption in God. Nothing short of a total death to self would content her. Practising the severest self-mortification, she strove after complete subjection of the affections, the intellect, and the will, to the law of Christ. Not that she found this easy of attainment, for she continued to pursue it amid much inward conflict. Never to lose the presence of God amid the frivolities of fashionable life in Paris was a task so much beyond her that she felt constrained to seek safety in flight. Even so, she had to struggle against the appeal made to her vanity by praise which her conversational gifts as well as her beauty and wealth did not fail to draw forth. " I was as if torn asunder," she says, " for on the outside my vanity dragged me, and within, the Divine love." Failing to obtain help from her confessors during this spiritual combat, Madame Guyon went to see Geneviève Granger, the prioress of the Benedictines in Paris, and poured the story of her frailties and struggles into a sympathetic ear. " This great soul," she writes, " restored me, and encouraged me to resume my former consecration." On the Magdalen's Day, 1672, she signed and sealed the following marriage-contract with the Holy Child Jesus : " I promise to take for my Spouse our Lord, the Child, and to give myself to Him for spouse, though unworthy." The only dowry of her spiritual marriage she asked for was that of " crosses, scorn, confusion, disgrace, and ignominy." The union between her own will and the Divine was thus definitely accomplished.

After living for two years in peculiar blessedness Madame Guyon entered into a state of " total privation," which lasted far longer. Her dismal experience she records in these words : " No longer was there for me a God, Husband, Father, Lover—if I dared to call Him so. There was only a rigorous Judge." To complete her desolation, even the monk whose words first touched her wrote refusing further correspondence. She had despaired of ever emerging from this painful state when she had occasion to write to Father la Combe, superior of the Bernabites at Tonon, in Savoy. She told him she had fallen from grace, but he assured her to the contrary, and on Magdalen's Day, 1680, she experienced deliverance from all her troubles. Thus renewed in spirit, and her husband having died in 1676, she began to face the question of her future. In 1680 she resolved with the approval of D'Aranthon, titular bishop of the diocese, to devote herself to religious work on the

confines of Geneva. Father la Combe was appointed her
spiritual director. During a short stay with the Ursulines
at Tonon she began to perceive that she was called to
promulgate the doctrine of entire sanctification through
faith in the Saviour, and that in particular God willed
through her instrumentality to lead Father la Combe
from the state of illumination into the way of simple faith.
Though ostensibly her director, he was in reality directed
by her, and having under her influence embraced the
doctrine of present sanctification through faith, began
openly to preach it. As it was no secret that Madame
Guyon was the real force behind this new movement, she
was instructed to confine herself to charitable work. The
emphasis laid by her upon the religion of the heart, and
the implied depreciation of outward forms and ceremonies,
together with her refusal to accede to his wishes, alienated
the good but vacillating bishop. She accordingly removed
in 1682 to the Ursuline convent at Tonon. Throughout
the two years she spent there she had much to endure at
the hands of the bishop, his ecclesiastic, the sisters at Gex,
the New Catholics, and her stepbrother Father la Mothe.
Her letters were intercepted, her doctrine denounced, and
her character aspersed. Nevertheless she enjoyed great
tranquillity of soul, being so lost in the will of God as to
will only what He willed. As Father la Combe had
espoused the cause of the new spiritualism, it was formally
represented to Bishop D'Aranthon that the interests of the
Church called for authoritative interference on his part ;
whereupon the facile bishop gave orders that both Madame
Guyon and la Combe should quit his diocese. This strong
measure shewed that whether or not Madame Guyon's
doctrinal tenets were out of keeping with the traditional
creed of the Roman Catholic Church, her spirit and her
sympathies were alien to her co-religionists of that time.

While yet at Tonon, she had begun to formulate her
doctrine of a " fixed state," attainable only through entire
devotion to God, and carrying with it absolute imperturba-
bility in the soul's central depth. In 1683 she wrote
Les Torrents, an original and attractive treatise embodying
her personal religious experience. Its purpose is to trace
the progressive development of the soul from the genesis
of its spiritual life to its perfect union with God. In

illustration of her theme she makes adroit use of the similitude of torrents, which, rising on the top of the mountains, roll on with varying speed and directness towards the ocean. This idea, apparently derived from Amos 5²⁴ (" Let judgement run down as waters, and righteousness as a mighty stream " = torrent), is applied to the delineation of the course of the inward life in a manner possible only to literary and imaginative powers of no mean order. *Les Torrents* is perhaps the finest product of Madame Guyon's pen, and affords ample evidence of her singular powers of spiritual perception.

In 1684 she took up residence in Grenoble, and began to write her commentaries on the Bible, and soon also became a recognized spiritual force throughout the neighbourhood. Chagrined that so much influence should be exercised by a *woman*, and alarmed at the stir created by the publication of her *Short and Easy Method of Prayer*, in which she urged the importance of inward recollection and respectful silence as compared with the constant use of articulate words, the ecclesiastical authorities were once more roused to antagonism. Although Bishop Camus of Grenoble shewed himself friendly to her, she decided to leave the city. During a brief stay at Vercelli she wrote upon the Apocalypse. The climate, however, proved unsuitable, and in 1686 she returned to Paris, where there was scope for the exercise of all her gifts. Within a year after her return to the capital, and just as her influence was making itself felt in aristocratic circles, an event took place which affected her whole future. This was the condemnation by the Inquisition at Rome of Molinos, the Spanish monk who, in his *Spiritual Guide*, taught that the way to Christ-perfection lay through complete indifference to external things and entire surrender of the will to God. Although the first attempt to arraign him in 1681 had failed, he was in 1687 declared a heretic and thrown into prison. As we have already had occasion to notice, the head and front of his offending lay not so much in his teaching itself as in its alleged injurious effect upon the public estimation of the Church and its ritual. By the condemnation of Molinos a welcome weapon was put into the hands of Father la Mothe and of the Provincial of the Bernabites of Paris, who were jealous of la Combe as a popular preacher. They represented him to the archbishop as sharing the erroneous propositions of Molinos. The result was that he was lodged in the Bastille, and afterwards shut up in a fortress for life.

La Mothe, a peculiarly contemptible and vindictive creature, now set himself to victimize his own sister. Baulked in his attempt to induce her to allay, by flight to Montargis, the apprehensions regarding her which he had done his best to create, and also in his proposal to become her spiritual director, and finding it impossible to impugn her moral character, he left no stone unturned to have her branded as a heretic. By falsely alleging that she was in correspondence with Molinos, by giving out that she had written a dangerous book, and by forging a letter from which it appeared that she was bent on holding religious assemblies at the houses of persons unknown to her, he secured from Louis XIV. a *lettre de cachet* authorizing her imprisonment. Though still kept in prison after four interrogations, she remained content and joyful. It was during this period of confinement that, at the instigation of la Combe, she wrote her fascinating autobiography. Although La Mothe had embittered against her the minds of the archbishop and the official, and still carried on his campaign of malicious calumny, aided by the manufacture of counterfeit documents, he was happily thwarted in his nefarious designs. A visitor to the Convent of St. Marie, impressed with the testimony borne by the prioress and the nuns, secured on Madame Guyon's behalf the good offices of the Court favourite, Madame de Maintenon, who persuaded the King to order that she should be set at liberty.

On her release Madame Guyon temporarily found a retreat in the house of Madame de Miramion, who had obtained for her the kindly interest of Madame de Maintenon. After some days, in the house of the Duchesse de Charost, to whom she had become related through the marriage of her daughter, she met that noble and illustrious man, the Abbé de Fénelon, and with this began another epoch in her history. A certain " union of spirit " led to written correspondence, and in the interchange of views thus effected the future Archbishop of Cambray was sensibly influenced by his new friend. Meanwhile the teaching of Madame Guyon was making some stir in Paris and its neighbourhood, and signs of opposition soon appeared. Indeed, during the whole of the two and a half years when she resided with her daughter, and also when she took a small secluded house for herself, her persecutors continued to torment her. Certain ecclesiastics were persuaded that the Church was endangered through the propagation of " the new spirituality " ; Peter Nicole, the Port-Royalist, expressed disapproval of her little treatise on Prayer ; even Madame de Maintenon abandoned her ; and in the end, Bossuet, Bishop of Meaux, took the field as her violent opponent. On her own suggestion at an interview with the latter in September 1693, all her writings, including her autobiography, were submitted to him for examination. Another conference was held in 1694. Although differing from her on several points, such as specific requests in prayer, the woman of the Apocalypse, the outflow of graces, the Apostolic state, and the stifling of distinct acts, the Bishop of Meaux admitted that these were matters which touched neither the faith nor the doctrine of the Church. He even offered to give her a certificate of general orthodoxy, but this she declined.

At this juncture, as it chanced, the public mind was further agitated by the issue of Nicole's *Refutation des Principales Erreurs des Quiétistes*. Finding that her morals as well as her creed were being widely aspersed, " this poor Quietist," as Wesley calls her, now wrote to Madame de Maintenon requesting that commissioners should be appointed to investigate her case. Madame de Maintenon declared herself satisfied with regard to her character, but thought that her doctrinal teaching should be thoroughly inquired into. This task was accordingly assigned to a commission of three—Bossuet, Tronson (superior of St. Sulpice), and De Noailles (Bishop of Chalons). At their desire she submitted to them all her books and manuscripts, and in order to lighten their labours, she also made a collection of extracts from Patristic and Mystic theologians which shewed that in her doctrinal position she was in accord with these approved authors. Her positive assertion that the Bishop of Meaux would never either read or allow the others to see those " Justifications " is at once pathetic and disappointing. At the first meeting of the commissioners Madame Guyon saw that, although " he had his good moments," she had been deceived in the idea she had formed of the Bishop of Meaux. Besides insisting on the exclusion of her friend the Duc de Chevreuse, whom she had asked to be present, he acted throughout as one who had resolved upon her condemnation. De Noailles shewed himself more considerate. Tronson expressed satisfaction with her straightforwardness. As Bossuet still had his misgivings, further conferences were held at Issi, with the result that certain " Articles " dealing with the doctrine of " pure love " were framed, and signed by her. When, however, the Bishop of Meaux demanded that she should formally declare herself a heretic by signing a pastoral letter in which he had specifically condemned certain current errors, he met with a firm refusal. During these proceedings Madame Guyon voluntarily entered and remained in a convent at Meaux, and on her departure for Paris the bishop handed her a certificate without asking her for any further signature. Her return to the capital was the signal for renewed agitation against her ; and Bossuet, realizing that the situation was viewed with displeasure in the highest quarters, and was therefore likely to affect adversely his own interests, now wrote asking that the certificate he had given her should be returned to him, and substituting one less favourable in its place. Her declinature to acquiesce led to an open rupture with the bishop and to fresh violence on the part of her adversaries generally. In December 1695 she was imprisoned at Vincennes, where she spent her time mostly in hymn-writing.

Bossuet now devoted himself to the study of the inner life and wrote his *Instructions sur les États d'Oraison*, submitting it before publication not only to De Noailles and the Bishop of Chartres, but also to the brilliant Fénelon who, in 1695, had been appointed Archbishop of Cambray, and with whom he had formed a close friendship. Fénelon withdrew his approval, not on the score of doctrine, but because of the unfair personal attack made upon Madame Guyon who also had become his friend. In vindication of his own position he published, in 1697, his *Maximes des Saints sur la Vie Intérieure*. Professedly an exposition of the views of approved authors on the subject of holy living, this was virtually a defence of the maligned lady. The course of this stirring controversy was marked by the issue of several treatises on the part of both combatants, and an excited public witnessed the spectacle of the two leading theologians of France at open variance. Having exposed himself not only to the opposition of Bossuet, but also to the suspicion of the King, rather than be untrue to his convictions as in some sense a disciple of Madame Guyon, Fénelon was banished from Court and, after much debate and hesitation, condemned at Rome on 12th March 1699. In accordance with the principles expressed in his *De Auctoritate*, which affirmed the Ultramontane conception of papal authority, he loyally submitted to the condemnation, which was, however, a modified one, and bore that certain propositions of his book were condemned, not in the sense in which they were explained by himself, but only in the sense which others put upon them. Throughout these painful proceedings Fénelon bore himself very nobly, and shewed himself to be in point of Christian character far superior to his illustrious antagonist. Madame Guyon had at an early stage perceived that his advocacy of her cause was fraught with probable injury to himself, but he magnanimously refused to believe it. Now that her prognostications had proved correct, he sustained his trials in a meek and quiet spirit, and pursued with tireless assiduity among the people of his diocese the works of Christian piety and benevolence. While he did not wholly accept Madame Guyon's views, the part played by Fénelon in the controversy to which they gave rise shews that he was not only convinced of the sincerity of her intentions, but was in reality himself a mystic. At the same time, from his remarkable versatility, he was so much more than a mystic that he can scarcely be classed with those whose mysticism is their distinguishing characteristic. In particular, he identified himself with Madame Guyon's assertion that love towards God is love for Himself irrespective of recompense, and that in the best Christians love takes precedence of every other grace. By some he was understood also to teach Perfectionism, and to exalt Quietistic contemplation in preference to fighting the good fight. In Madame Guyon and Fénelon, Mysticism in France had its two last weighty representatives. Not without reason it has been held that by condemning them the Church appeared to abandon their perhaps somewhat sombre point of view only to plunge into the current of a worldly materialism from which probably it had never quite emerged.

After being shut up at Vincennes for eight months, Madame Guyon was imprisoned for two years at Vaugirard, and then taken in 1698 to the Bastille, where she remained for four years. In 1702 she was liberated and banished to Blois. She was now fifty-four years of age, and reduced by sufferings to a feeble state of health. Many pious people visited her in the place of her banishment, where, as she had opportunity, she continued to witness for God until, on 9th June 1717, she died in simple reliance on the Lord Jesus Christ.

By general consent Madame Guyon figures as a notable woman. She was distinguished alike for her physical beauty, her powers of intellect and imagination, and her rare spirituality of character. To think of her merely as an erratic and restless visionary, or as a fanatical dreamer, is to do her serious injustice. Even Wesley, who had no love for Quietists, refuses to regard her so. " I believe," he says, " Madame Guyon was in several mistakes, speculative and practical too. Yet I would no more dare to call her than her friend, Archbishop Fénelon, ' a distracted enthusiast.' " She was undoubtedly a woman of a very uncommon understanding and of excellent piety. Nor was she any more " a lunatic " than she was " a heretic." Although not a stylist like Teresa, she wrote well both in prose and verse. Along with an alert mind she had a large heart. Perfectly free from that inordinate love of money which characterized her fellow-Quietist, Madame Bourignon, she was capable of the most generous and self-denying deeds. While deeply and even passionately attached to her Church, her life was a strong protest against the prevailing externalism and ecclesiasticism of her age, hence her collision with the official authorities and ruling powers. Teresa, whose energies were devoted to the building-up of the outward fabric of the Church, was canonized ; Madame Guyon, whose influence tended to magnify the importance of the inner life of the soul and to relegate to a secondary place the ceremonial and institu-

6

tional side of religion, had bitter waters of a full cup wrung out to her. Amid the persecution and calumniation to which she was so long subjected, she maintained on the whole a calmness and patience of demeanour, a sweetness of disposition, and a Christian humility possible only to a highly sanctified soul. History has to record few more shining examples of ceaseless devotion to the cause of heart-religion than that associated with the name of Madame Guyon. Hers was eminently a life of faith and prayer and entire consecration to the Divine will—a life that seemed to move between the two poles of rapt communion with God and disinterested love for the souls of men.

SELECTIONS FROM THE WRITINGS OF MADAME GUYON

(1) *Autobiography*

" God does not establish His great works except upon ' the nothing.' It seems that He destroys in order to build. He does it so in order that this temple He destines for Himself, built even with much pomp and majesty, but built none the less by the hand of men, should be previously so destroyed that there remains not one stone upon another. It is these frightful ruins which will be used by the Holy Spirit to construct a Temple which will not be built by the hand of men, but by His power alone."

" The absence of the cross was for me so terrible a cross, that the desire for its return made me languish, and led me to say, like St. Teresa, ' Either to suffer or to die ? ' It was not slow in returning, this charming cross, and the strange thing was that, though I desired it so vehemently, when it returned, it appeared to me so heavy and burdensome, it was almost insupportable."

" O Infinite Goodness, Thou wert so near, and I went running here and there to look for Thee, and I did not find Thee. My life was miserable, and my happiness was within me. I was in poverty in the midst of riches, and I was dying of hunger near a table spread and a continual feast. It was for want of understanding those words of Thy Gospel when Thou sayest, ' The kingdom of God is not here or there, but the kingdom of God is within you.' "

" Visions are in the powers inferior to the will, and their effect must always terminate at the will, and in the sequel they must be lost in the experience of what one sees, knows, and hears in those states ; otherwise the soul would never arrive at the perfect union. What she would then have that she would even give the name of union to, would be a mediated union, and a flowing of the gifts of God into the powers ; but it is not God Himself. . . . The vision is never of God Himself, nor almost ever of Jesus Christ, as those who have them imagine. It is an angel of light, who, according to the power which is given him by God, causes the soul to see His representation, which he himself takes."

" Ecstasy comes from a sensible delight which is a spiritual sensuality, where the soul, letting herself go too far, in consequence of the sweetness she finds there, falls into faintness. The devil gives this kind of sensible sweetness to entice the soul, make her hate the cross, to render her sensual, and to fill her with vanity and love of self, to arrest her at the gifts of God, and to hinder her from following Jesus Christ by renunciation and death to all things."

" I used to place myself in a corner, where I worked. I could hardly do anything from the strength of the attraction, which made the work fall from my hands. I passed hours in this way, without being able either to open my eyes or know what was going on in me, which was so simple, so peaceful, so sweet, that I sometimes said to myself, ' Is heaven more peaceful than I ? ' "

" I had no need of resigning myself and submitting. . . . It seemed to me it would have been impossible to will anything but what Thou wert doing in me. If I had a will, it appeared to me that it was with Thine, like two lutes in perfect accord ; that which is not touched gives forth the same sound as the one touched ; it is only one same sound and one single harmony. It is this union of the will which establishes the soul in perfect peace."

" It seemed to me that I had in Jesus Christ all that was wanting to me in myself. I was, O Divine Jesus, that lost sheep of the house of Israel, that Thou wert come to save. Thou wert truly the Saviour of her who could find no salvation out of Thee. O man, strong and holy, find salvation as much as you please in what you have done, that is holy and glorious for God ; as for me, I make my boast only in my weaknesses, since they have earned for me such a Saviour."

"A bone dislocated and out of the place where the economy of Divine wisdom had placed it, does not cease to give pain until it is back again in its natural order. Whence come so many troubles, so many conflicts ? It is that the soul has not been willing to remain in her place, nor to content herself with what she has and what happens to her from moment to moment. It is the same in the order of grace as in that of nature."

(2) *A Short and Easy Method of Prayer*

"It is by prayer alone that we are brought into this (God's) presence, and maintained in it without interruption. You must then learn a species of prayer, which may be exercised at all times ; which doth not obstruct outward employments ; and which may be equally practised by princes, kings, prelates, priests, and magistrates, soldiers, and children, tradesmen, labourers, women and sick persons ; it cannot, therefore, be the prayer of the head, but of the heart ; not a prayer of the understanding alone, which is so limited in its operations that it can have but one object at one time ; but the prayer of the heart is not interrupted by the exercises of reason : indeed nothing can interrupt this prayer, but irregular and disordered affections ; and when once we have tasted of God, and the sweetness of His love, we shall find it impossible to relish aught but Himself."

" 'The Lord is in his holy temple, let all the earth keep silence before him ' (Hab 2²⁰). Inward silence is absolutely indispensable, because the Word is essential and eternal, and necessarily requires dispositions in the soul in some degree correspondent to His nature, as a capacity for the reception of Himself. Hearing is a sense formed to receive sounds, and is rather passive than active, admitting, but not communicating, sensation ; and if we would hear, we must bend the ear for that purpose : so

Christ, the eternal Word, without whose Divine inspeaking the soul is dead, dark, and barren, when He would speak within us, requires the most silent attention to His all-quickening and efficacious voice. . . . The Spirit of God needs none of our arrangements and methods ; when it pleaseth Him, He turns shepherds into prophets, and so far from excluding any from the Temple of Prayer, He throws wide the gates, that all may enter."

(3) *Spiritual Torrents*

" You will observe that some rivers move more gravely and slowly, and others with greater velocity ; but there are rivers and *torrents* which rush with frightful impetuosity, and which nothing can arrest. It is thus with souls. Some go on quietly towards perfection, and never reach the sea, or only very late, contented to lose themselves in some stronger and more rapid river, which carries them with itself into the sea. Others, which form the second class, flow on more vigorously and promptly than the first. They even carry with them a number of rivulets ; but they are slow and idle in comparison with the last class, which rush onward with so much impetuosity, that they are utterly useless : they are not available for navigation, nor can any merchandise be trusted upon them, except at certain parts and at certain times. . . . The second class are more agreeable and more useful ; their gravity is pleasing, they are all laden with merchandise, and we sail upon them without fear or peril."

B. *PROTESTANT*

I. GERMAN MYSTICS

Jacob Boehme as Chief Representative

German Mysticism sprang up in the wake of the mystical pantheism originating in Erigena and brought into practice by Amalric. The way for its introduction had been prepared in numerous thirteenth-century convents, and by the Béguines, who at the commencement of the fourteenth century were practically identical with the pantheistic Brethren of the Free Spirit. These factors, combined with the co-operation of various women's associations in closer connexion with the Church, helped to swell the tide of mysticism. All alike were animated by a spirit of genuine piety, and called for the reform of prevalent abuses in the Church. Although Eckhart had no outward connexion with the Brethren, and expressly repudiated their heretical doctrines, his influence told in the same direction, owing to the stress laid by him on the necessity of inward contemplation in order to the satisfaction of the deepest longings of the soul. Account must also be taken of the calamitous situation—political, economic, and social —of Germany in the first half of the fourteenth century. Louis of Bavaria and Frederick of Austria were rival claimants for the imperial crown. Louis was victorious, but in 1324 was put under interdict by Pope John XXII., who claimed the right of decision. In 1327, however, Louis was crowned at Rome and appointed a rival pope, but only to call forth fresh denunciations from Avignon. Germany suffered heavily from inverted seasons, oppressive exactions, and social disorder fanned by fanatical persecution of the Jews and the fury of the Flagellants. Her people were also the victims at once of war and famine, floods and pestilence (the Black Death). In such a bitter sea of troubles the religious mind sought consolation not in the observance of outward rites or penances, but in the endeavour to gain internal peace. Those thus disposed retired within the soul itself, became pupils in the school of suffering, formed the united brotherhood of the " Friends of God," and devoted themselves to loving imitation of Christ in earnest aspiration after the attainment of His Deity. As already stated, they were largely disciples of Eckhart, and amongst them were numbered both Suso and Tauler. Mysticism, in fact, now found in Germany its principal point of concentration.

In his monumental work on *The History of Dogma*, Adolf Harnack says : " By Mysticism there is to be understood nothing but *theological piety* (contemplation) . . . ; there are no national or confessional distinctions in it. . . . Mysticism is the Catholic expression of individual piety in general. . . . If Protestantism is not at some time yet . . . to become entirely mystical, it will never be possible to make Mysticism Protestant without flying in the face of history and Catholicism." [1] It may seem rash to question so great an authority, and the term " Protestant Mysticism " is perhaps to some extent a misnomer, but the thing it stands for, namely, the existence of mysticism among those outside of the Roman Catholic Church can hardly be challenged " without "—to retort Harnack's assertion against himself—" flying in the face of history " and Protestantism. Jacob Boehme and William Law were both mystics, but must they therefore be ranked as Catholics ? On the contrary they were Protestants, and why should they not be suitably called Protestant mystics ? It is merely the statement of a fact, and implies nothing more. Moreover, to designate the one a German, and the other an English mystic, is not necessarily to say that there is any difference in respect of their mysticism as such and in itself. Although, then, according to Harnack, Mysticism is to be regarded as exclusively Catholic, this judgement must be considered too sweeping. The distinguished author commands assent, however, when he writes : " In the fifteenth century the currents of all foregoing attempts at reform flowed together ; they could converge into *one* channel, for *all* of them sprang originally from one source—the doctrine of poverty, wedded to apocalyptic and to certain Augustinian thoughts—that is, Catholicism." [2] Protestants, of course, there were not yet. The time of the Mendicant monks was marked by a lofty religious tone, which was one of the several converging tributaries to the growing current of reforming zeal mentioned by Harnack. It was the teaching of the Church that, to become nothing so as to realize union with God, one must be an imitator of Christ and accept the historical Scriptures. But the idea of *imitation* had been pushed to the point of extravagance indicated in the notion that " one must become a Christ one's self." The Church mystics were unable to control this wild type of piety, which had indeed received some stimulus from Aquinas himself, and afterwards, among others, from Eckhart. The idea that in the soul there is a Divine element or " spark," became with many a kind of obsession, and pantheism was submerged in the sense not only of self-consequence, but even of self-deification.

[1] Vol. vi. p. 97 ff. in Eng. tr.   [2] *Ibid.* p. 115.

In one important direction the reformation of the Church was largely promoted by the Mendicant Orders, whose members adopted and advocated the practice of self-denying brotherly love as the real test of a living Christianity among monks and laymen alike. No longer, as under the old monasticism, was beneficent aid to a poor brother considered a work of supererogation. Rather was it deemed a service so obligatory that, in order to its performance, Eckhart advised his followers to sacrifice ecstasy itself. The seed sown by Francis of Assisi, and fostered by Aquinas, Bonaventura, and many later mystics, was bearing fruit for two or three centuries before the Reformation. Monks and laity were brought into closer touch; the spirit of charity was awakened; and the free Christian societies, especially in Germany, grew apace.

The " German " mystic movement dates from the end of the thirteenth century. It is described by Harnack as " the introduction of the impassioned individual piety of the monastic theologians into the circles of the laity." [1] This work, the nature of which finds illustration in the labours and writings of Eckhart and Tauler, Suso and Ruysbroek, and in the activities of the " Friends," was mainly carried out by Dominican monks. According to the Thomist mystics the soul can already here below attain to full and rapturous fellowship with God—an experience which is the fruit of perfect knowledge conveyed in vision. They still stressed the importance of the intellect. The Scotists or Nominalists, again, with increasing success, contended that salvation lies in the union with God effected by the surrender of the human will to the Divine. Although in many ways the fabric of the mediæval world was crumbling towards dissolution, there was no determination to break away from what Thomas à Kempis calls " the sound doctrine of the Church." Widespread dissatisfaction with her corruptions did not mean repudiation of her dogmas, which as yet included no pronouncements concerning such thorny questions as indulgences, freewill, and hierarchical pretensions. It was against her official representatives for the time being, against unworthy priests and indolent monks, against her institutions, political and ecclesiastical,

[1] *Op. cit.* vol. vi. p. 113 of Eng. tr.

that active hostility was developed.   The revolution that was imminent menaced indeed the Church's institutions, but not her gospel.   Except in point of greater reality and vigour, the new piety did not in fact differ from the old.

In his valuable and suggestive treatise on *Communion with God* the Ritschlian Herrmann practically agrees with Harnack in viewing mysticism as the exclusive possession of the Roman Catholic Church.   Starting from the position that its most conspicuous features are " obedience to the laws of cultus and of doctrine on the one side and Neo-platonic mysticism on the other," he asserts that " it is in these alone that we may see and study the kind of religion which is characteristic of Roman Catholicism," and that " he who seeks in this wise that for which he is ready to abandon all beside, has stepped beyond the pale of Christian piety.   He leaves Christ's kingdom altogether behind him when he enters that sphere of experience which seems to him to be the highest. . . . For the fact that everything historical sinks into insignificance when God is really found may so dominate the will of the individual that he may become totally indifferent to the doctrine of the importance of the historical in Christianity." [1]   These quotations sufficiently indicate the standpoint of the writer.   As a Christian theologian he considers mysticism to be a feature of religious life peculiar to Roman Catholicism, and declares that any retention of it by Pro-testants is a capitulation to Catholic dogma.   He thus rejects the widely held view that mysticism is common to religion in general, and treats it as in itself " a particular species of religion " which dispenses with the historical as an irksome drag.   To this critic mysticism is wholly objectionable, but chiefly (1) because it has nothing more definite to say of God than that He is utterly different from the world ;   (2) because it tends to drift into pantheistic metaphysics ;   (3) because it belittles Christ by making Him merely a preparatory step leading to God Himself as the true goal.   At the climax of life, along with all external things, Christ is dismissed from the soul, and the true conception of Him as the revelation of God in history is destroyed.

Even allowing that there is considerable justification

[1] Book i. ch. i., Eng. tr.

for these charges, and without entering upon any detailed discussion of them, we may still ask—(1) Is Hermann right in saying that " mysticism is not that which is common to all religion, but a particular species of religion ? " [1] And, if so, is he quite consistent with himself in making the further statement that " in mysticism the universal aim of all religion is clearly grasped ? " Can he have it both ways ? (2) Is there no such thing as *Christian* mysticism ? Leading authorities on the subject do not hesitate to use the term ; Dr. Inge even adopts it as the title of his excellent book. Were the mystics of the Roman Church before the Reformation—Bernard, Suso, Tauler, and the rest—not Christians ? And are we to deny the name to post-Reformation mystics, whether Catholic like Teresa and De Sales, or Protestant like Boehme and William Law ? Surely this cannot be done. (3) Again, it may be asked, have the mystics rendered no service to Christianity ? Is it not a well-attested fact that, in spite of the criticisms that may fairly be passed upon them, in spite of their defects, errors, and even absurdities, they have not only vindicated their title to be called Christians, but have also performed a notable service in counteracting the petrifying influence of an arid scholasticism which threatened to prove fatal to the very existence of real piety ? Herrmann admits that in " the excellent treatise of S. Dénifle " [2] the Protestant Christian will find much to his edification, and that apart from the Scriptures Richard Rothe could think of no better aid to devotion than the writings of the mystics. Are we then as Protestants to question the genuineness of all Roman Catholic piety, and to count it at best as a fine expression of a particular species of religion ? (4) Finally, if mysticism is to be entirely banned, must not the Protestant Christian be prepared servilely to subject his religious life to the authoritative yoke of ecclesiastical dogma ? If the soul is to prosper and be in health, must it not breathe the fresh air of the Spirit, of contemplation, meditation, and prayer ?

The most notable among post-Reformation non-Catholic

[1] Book i. ch. i. p. 22, Eng. tr.

[2] *The Spiritual Life* ; or, Flowers gathered from the Gardens of the German Mystics and " Friends of God " of the Fourteenth Century. Third edition, 1880.

mystics was Jacob Boehme—or Behmen, as he is often styled in English—(1575–1624). Belonging to a substantial peasant family, and apprenticed at the age of fourteen to a shoemaker, he afterwards became a master workman, and practised his craft at Görlitz, where he purchased a house and settled as a married man. Imbued from early boyhood with a deep religious sense of God in nature, he thought on independent lines, and already in his earlier writings showed a special bent towards philosophical mysticism. Owing, however, to a copy of the manuscript of his first work, *The Aurora; or, Morning Dawn*, which he never intended to publish, having furtively come under the notice of Gregory Richter, primarius preacher and local superior at Görlitz, this fanatical and arrogant pedant set himself to subject the poor cobbler to a bitter persecution, in which he induced the town authorities to bear a part. Although a sentence of banishment passed upon him as " a villain full of piety " was speedily revoked, Boehme was forbidden to write any more books. Falling thus under the ban of the civil and ecclesiastical powers, he published nothing for several years, but after this interval he could no longer refrain from writing, and again began to issue various treatises from the press. As a result he was driven into exile, returning from retirement at Dresden in his fiftieth year only to die. This practically sums up the meagre biography of this philosophic and devotional thinker. Apart from personal references scattered throughout his works— something like thirty in number—there are no further events in his life to chronicle. Numerous tales were current in his day illustrative of his humility and meekness of disposition, and his gift of discerning spirits. These were perhaps of a somewhat legendary character, but there is sufficient evidence to show that he exhibited many pure and noble qualities.

Already in the *Aurora*, Boehme tells how, overwhelmed by life's mystery, sin, and misery, he raised his heart to God, and seemed suddenly to be embraced by the Divine arms. " I can compare it," he writes, " to nothing else but the resurrection at the last day. For then, with all reverence I say it, with the eye of my spirit I saw God. I saw both what God is, and I saw how God is what He is.

And with that there came a mighty and incontrollable
impulse to set down so as to preserve what I had seen."
Destitute as this work is of literary merit, it reveals more
truly perhaps than any of his other treatises the real
Boehme. At the outset it may be premised that he claims
to write only what he had seen by Divine illumination.
He expressly adds, however : " Let it never be imagined
that I am any greater or any better than other men.
When the Spirit of God is taken away from me, I cannot
even read so as to understand what I have myself written.
. . . I marvel every day that God should reveal both
the Divine Nature and Temporal and Eternal Nature for
the first time to such a simple and unlearned man as I am.
But what am I to resist what God will do ? What am I
to say but, Behold the son of thine handmaiden ! . . .
The gate of the Divine mystery was sometimes so opened
to me that in one quarter of an hour I saw and knew
more than if I had been many years together at a university. . . . For I saw and knew the Being of all beings ;
the Byss and the Abyss,[1] as, also, the Generation of the
Son and the Procession of the Spirit. I saw the descent
and original of this world also, and of all its creatures. I
saw in their order and outcome the Divine world, the
angelical world, paradise, and then this fallen and dark
world of our own. I saw the beginning of the good and
the evil, and the true origin and existence of each of
them. . . . And then it came with commanding power
into my mind that I must set down the same in pen and
ink for a memorial to myself ; albeit I could hardly contain
or express what I had seen. For twelve years this went
on in me. Sometimes the truth would hit me like a sudden
smiting storm of rain ; and then there would be the clear
sunshine after the rain. All which was to teach me that
God will manifest Himself in the soul of man after what
manner and what measure it pleases Him and as it seems
good in His sight."

[1] Compare with this what Angela of Foligno says in her *Visionum
et Instructionum Liber*, c. 22 : " I had comprehension of the whole
world, both here and beyond the sea, and the Abyss and all things
else ; and therein I beheld naught save the divine power in a
manner which is verily indescribable, so that through greatness of
marvelling the soul cried with a loud voice, saying, ' This whole
world is full of God.' "

Boehme's second work was entitled *The Three Principles of the Divine Essence*. In this he treats of God, Nature, and Man, and also of heaven and hell. To him God is at once within the world and above it, but neither within it in the pantheistic sense of being merely the soul of the world developing itself in time by a necessary process, nor in the theistic sense of merely reigning in the remote heaven and not dwelling among his creatures. While not identifying Nature with God, he holds that " He Himself is all, and communicates His power to all His works." The Eternal Nature is not the medium of creation ; for God no medium is necessary, seeing that with Him to think is at the same time to realize. Man's destiny depends on himself. We may either follow or extinguish the divinely given inner light of the Spirit, and so reach our paradise or the reverse. In *The Threefold Life of Man*, which followed, he insists that its serviceableness to any reader will be proportionate to his individual complexion and condition. The next work of our prolific author was that containing his famous answers to the *Forty Questions* submitted to him by a certain Balthazar Walter, who had journeyed far and wide in search of occult wisdom, and informed himself regarding the main philosophical and theological problems canvassed at the German universities in those days. This man became his ardent disciple, and it is interesting to find that even the son of his persecutor, Richter, helped to circulate his writings. Next in order came *A Treatise of the Incarnation of the Son of God*. The subject, he says, would require an angel's pen, but as the pen of a sinner's love he claims that his own is better. In the *Signatura Rerum* (1621) he represents the visible world as a symbol of the invisible, as the outward form of an invisible essence. This is true alike of nature and of man, the hidden spirit being revealed in the signature of the outward form. Everything in heaven or earth can be discovered in the minor world of man. Fantastically enough, the facts of the evangelical narrative are interwoven with chemical and astronomical matter as, for example, thus : " Adam had brought his will into the poison of the external Mercury. So, then, must Christ, as Love, yield up his will also in the venomous Mercury. Adam ate of the evil tree ; Christ must eat of the wrath of God ; and as it came to

pass inwardly in the spirit, so must it also outwardly in
the flesh. . . . Mercury, in the philosophic work, signifieth
the Pharisees, who cannot endure the dear child."

In *The Way to Christ*, composed of four tracts dealing
in turn with True Repentance, True Resignation, Regeneration, and The Supersensual Life, Boehme draws largely
upon his own experience. Of the last-mentioned tract, as
beautifully translated by William Law, Dr. Alexander
Whyte says it is " a superb piece of spiritual work, and a
treasure-house of masculine English." Boehme's next
work was *A Treatise of the Four Complexions* (= Tempera-
ments). In the sub-title it is called " A Consolatory Instruction for a Sad and Assaulted Heart." It displays a
profound knowledge of the human heart, especially as
regards his own temperament—that of melancholy. " I
know well myself," he says, " what melancholy is. I also
have lodged all my days in the melancholy inn." This
treatise is particularly remarkable as comprising the
philosophy of temptation. Passing over Boehme's con-
troversial and apologetic writings, we note next his treatise
on *Election*, ch. viii. of which he devotes to " The
Sayings of Scripture, and how they oppose one another,"
and ch. ix. to " Clearing the Right Understanding of such
Scriptures," his aim being to harmonize apparently con-
tradictory passages. Characteristically, in an *Appendix
on Repentance*, he seeks to make his own and his reader's
calling and election sure.

The *Mysterium Magnum* elaborates the view that the
ideas of the Divine wisdom take on an outward form in
the Eternal Nature, the one being conceived as the Maiden
and the other as the Mother of the Universe. In this
treatise Boehme allegorizes, spiritualizes, and interprets of
Christ the entire Book of Genesis. With reference to the
mysticism and penetrating allegorism of this extensive
work, Dr. Whyte says that " Philo himself is a tyro and a
timid interpreter beside Jacob Behmen." In some respects
this is perhaps a doubtful compliment, although one cannot
but be impressed with the declaration of Schopenhauer,
quoted by the same authority : " When I read Behmen's
book, I cannot withhold either admiration or emotion."
Boehme died leaving several works in a fragmentary
condition, including *A Treatise on Baptism and the Lord's*

Supper; *Theoscopiæ, or Divine Wisdom,* containing a discussion of various problems, philosophical and religious; and *Holy Week*. Even as it stands, the last named is a valuable aid to devotion, and shows what a rich vein of practical piety underlies all his speculative philosophy and theological conceptions. Very evidently he not only knew, but daily and hourly practised, the apostolic precept: " Pray without ceasing." All his thoughts were bathed in prayer.

Acquainted with no books except the Bible, the works of Paracelsus, and a few other writings of a theosophic and alchemistic cast, Boehme may be said in general to have aimed, under the influence of symbolism thence derived, and with the aid of a poetic imagination and images drawn from nature, at setting forth philosophical notions of a distinctly novel description. His work will always be valuable as following up the attempt of Valentine Weigel (1533–88) to combine the older subjective mysticism with the new objective mysticism and symbolism. Weigel directs him to retire into himself and passively await the entrance of the Divine Word, and assures him that through the indwelling of God he is already in Paradise. Paracelsus declares that with the Bible alone, and through the fulness of the Spirit, he may become wiser than the learned. By both he is led to believe that the key to the mysteries of outward nature is the disclosure by Divine enlightenment of the possibilities of our being. He takes refuge in the doctrine handed on by Sebastian Frank to Paracelsus, and by him to Weigel, namely, that of Divine manifestation by Contraries, and earnestly sets himself to search for a higher unity in which these might be harmonized, especially in their application to theology.

Although Boehme was far from being a systematic theologian, and although much obscurity attaches to his doctrinal position, his idea of God and the world can be stated with some measure of clearness. While accepting the standpoint of the Reformers with respect to sin and salvation through the redemptive work of Christ, he promulgated a higher doctrine of Godhead than Alexandria, Rome, or Geneva ever knew. To him it was given to qualify the abstruse metaphysic of the Athanasian creed by a strong assertion of the Eternal Love as an attribute of the

living God. In other words, he infuses into his conception
of God an element of the highest value—that of sympathy
with the heart of man, whereby through the consciousness
of the Divine love there is awakened a responsive love in
the human soul. A bridge is thus thrown over the gulf
between God and man, by which they are brought into
close and living contact and their essential kinship revealed.
It is a striking doctrine of the Godhead which is thus un-
folded. The distinction drawn by Boehme between the
Divine Nature or the Eternal Godhead and Eternal Nature
or the constituent ground out of which all the worlds,
visible and invisible, are made, interesting as it is, cannot
be expounded or discussed in this brief survey. Professedly
the mysteries of Deity were revealed to him in an ecstasy.
The Divine exterior to us, he maintains, can be conceived
only through the Divine *in* us. Divesting ourselves of all
self-will, we must in deepest lowliness yield ourselves up
to the Spirit of God, so that in His light we may see light.
His main proposition is that all creation proceeds from
God " by His self-differentiation into a negation of Himself," the peace of Unity thus passing into the strife of the
Manifold.   God manifests Himself in *contraries*.   In his
view, derived from Paracelsus, all things consist in Yes and
No, and the conflict between them is a fundamental law of
being.   This antithesis he represents as existing even in
the hidden life of the unmanifested Godhead and causing
an urge towards manifestation.   To use the words of Dr.
Inge : " As feeling this desire, the Godhead becomes
' Darkness.' The light which illumines the darkness is
the Son.   The resultant is the Holy Spirit, in whom arise
the archetypes of creation.   So he explains Body, Soul, and
Spirit as thesis, antithesis, and synthesis ; and the same
formula serves to explain Good, Evil, and Freewill, anger,
devils, and the world." [1]   Boehme's theosophy is thus
primarily linked up with the problem regarding the origin
of evil.   In its manifestation the Divine unity separates
into two principles—Good and Evil.   There is in everything
both good and evil, and evil is necessary to make good
clearly visible.   The bitter and the sweet, as manifested
in the creatures emanating from God, are, he holds, har-
moniously reunited by regeneration and obedience to the

[1] *Op. cit.* p. 279.

command, " Love thy neighbour as thyself." But what neither Boehme nor any other has been able to shew is how there can possibly be any harmony between two things mutually destructive. This might, for example, be done as between fortitude and meekness, but not as between good and evil, which completely cancel each other. His statements concerning evil are not always consistent, but there is no dubiety about his view that the entire cosmic process tends toward the ultimate triumph of good over evil.

Of sin Boehme strikingly says : " If all trees were clerks, and all their branches pens, and all the hills books, and all the water ink, yet all would not sufficiently declare the evil that sin hath done." In view of this he urges the sinner to throw himself upon the love of the Father, who will graciously welcome him. Laying great emphasis on the indwelling presence of Christ, he opposes the doctrine of imputed righteousness, maintaining that if the sacrifice of Christ " is to avail for me, it must be wrought in me." " That man," he says, " is no Christian who doth merely comfort himself with the suffering, death, and satisfaction of Christ, and doth impute it to himself as a gift of favour, remaining still himself a wild beast, and unregenerate. . . . I say, therefore, that no show of grace imputed from without can make a true Christian. Sin is not forgiven him by the speaking of a word once for all from without, as a lord of this world may give a murderer his life by an out-ward act of favour. No, this availeth nothing with God." He asserts, too, that heaven and hell are already in every human heart. Both are within us. To work together with God is to be in heaven ; to live the life of a bad man is to be in hell. And so with regard to the future state his teaching is that the soul, when freed from the trammels of the body, naturally finds its own place; " for where the body dies, there is heaven and hell. God is there, and the devil ; yea, each in his own kingdom. There also is Paradise ; and the soul needeth only to enter through the deep door in the centre."

Boehme's influence has been reflected not so much in the field of philosophical development as in the realm of religious experience and spiritual aspiration. His uncouth High Dutch style is by no means always lucid, and it is

7

not surprising that very varied and even completely diverse estimates have been made of his work. According to Bishop Warburton, " Behmen's works would disgrace Bedlam at full moon," while John Wesley characterizes them as " inimitable bombast." More judicial is the verdict of Henry More : " As for Jacob Behmen I do not see but that he holds firm the fundamentals of the Christian religion, and that his mind was devoutly united to the Head of the Church, the crucified Jesus, to whom he breathed out this short ejaculation with much fervency of spirit upon his deathbed : ' Thou crucified Lord Jesus, have mercy on me, and take me into Thy kingdom.' " Distinctly favourable judgements are not lacking. His remarkable speculative genius, combined with an almost unique vein of poetic imagination has caused him to be reckoned by German philosophers " the father of Protestant Mysticism." It is the affirmation of Professor Kurtz that " in speculative power and poetic wealth, exhibited with epic and dramatic effect, his system surpasses anything of the kind ever written." The Danish Bishop Martensen considers his visions of God and Nature and Man to be practically true. F. D. Maurice calls him " a generative thinker." William Law, a very clear and sober writer, was a keen disciple of " the blessed Behmen." " Next to the Scriptures," he says, " my only book is the illuminated Behmen." And Dr. Whyte, an ardent admirer of William Law, has also in a published lecture on " Jacob Behmen " paid cordial tribute to the Görlitz cobbler, whom he adjudges to be " of the race of the seers, and he stands out a very prince among them. He is full of eyes, and all his eyes are full of light." In this writer's opinion, " Wesley and others call names at Jacob Behmen, because they have not taken the trouble to learn his language, to master his mind, and to drink in his spirit."

In spite of recognized defects in Boehme—his verbose and turgid style, his impetuous vehemence, his singular nomenclature, his speculative and theosophic extravagances, his incoherent jumbling together of chemical and astrological processes with religious truth, his obscure and unsystematic theology—he certainly rendered signal service by his sincere endeavour to quicken the spiritual life of the Church of the Reformation, and to furnish it with a philosophic basis. Steadily shining through the cloud of his chimerical notions is the clear light of an appeal to the human heart to surrender itself to God.

It will be observed that in Germany Mysticism took on an aspect in marked contrast to that which it assumed in France. Not feeling, but abstract thought was its ruling characteristic. Unintelligibility was considered no drawback, and studious seclusion was preferred to the glitter of fashionable society. It is not overstating the case to say that, influential as Boehme became in Germany, he would have made but little impression in France. In the sprightly mentality of that country no literary production could win esteem if lacking in lucidity and liveliness.

It should further be noted that in one respect Protestant Mysticism as a whole presents a decided contrast to that of those who championed the counter-Reformation. As a rule, the Romanist looked upon his mystical experience as a peculiar privilege, and as something too sacred to be unveiled. In his eyes the transitory vision was a sign of special favour to himself, and to be treasured as such. Exceptionally, on the requisition of her confessor, Teresa wrote her life, with minute details of her spiritual record, although regarding the extraordinary bodily effects upon her of a state of rapture she had in vain prayed that these particulars might not be divulged. Not so the Protestant mystic. Any revelation vouchsafed to him he treated as a message to be handed on to others, with a view to their highest good and a practical reformation in their lives. He was not at all disposed to put his light " under a bushel."

The following extract from Boehme's *Dialogues on the Supersensual Life* is quoted by William James in illustration of the paradoxical style so much in vogue among mystical writers, and also of " the dialectical use, by the intellect, of negation as a mode of passage towards a higher kind of affirmation." Concerning the Primal Love, Boehme writes :

" It may fitly be compared to Nothing, for it is deeper than any Thing, and is as nothing with respect to all things, forasmuch as it is not comprehensible by any of them. And because it is nothing respectively, it is therefore free from all things, and is that only good,

which a man cannot express or utter what it is, there being
nothing to which it may be compared, to express it by.

"Love is Nothing, for when thou art gone forth wholly
from the Creature and from that which is visible, and art
become Nothing to all that is Nature and Creature, then
thou art in that eternal One, which is God Himself, and
then thou shalt feel within thee the highest virtue of
Love. . . . The treasure of treasures for the soul is where
she goeth out of the Somewhat into that Nothing out of
which all things may be made.   The soul here saith, *I
have nothing*, for I am utterly stripped and naked ; *I can do
nothing*, for I have no manner of power, but am as water
poured out ; *I am nothing*, for all that I am is no more
than an image of Being, and only God is to me I AM ; and
so, sitting down in my own Nothingness, I give glory to
the eternal Being, and *will nothing* of myself, that so God
may will all in me, being unto me my God and all things."

2. ENGLISH MYSTICS

(1) *The Cambridge Platonists*

It has been usual to distinguish between three classes of
Mystics—the speculative, the devotional, and the spiritualist.   In spite of some inevitable overlapping, the classifica-
tion may be adopted as fairly correct, care being taken,
however, not to misinterpret the term spiritualist.   Properly this signifies " Nature Mystic "—to use Dr. Inge's
definition—and has nothing to do with the degenerate
cult of clairvoyance, spirit rappings, theurgy, or any species
of magic.

Of special importance for speculative mysticism is the
illustrious name of Plato, which " appears and reappears
in cycles or waves of human thought all down the centuries.
Some of these are directly connected with Mysticism." [1]
To this category belong not only the earlier and later
Neoplatonists, but also the seventeenth-century Cambridge
Platonists.

The restoration of the monarchy in England witnessed
a marked decline in religion and morals.   Dignitaries of
the Church lived in luxury, while many of the ordinary

---

[1] E. C. Gregory, *op. cit.* p. 16.

clergy were apathetic and "at ease in Sion." To an appreciable extent, however, the credit of the Church was saved by the group of philosophical divines who flourished at Cambridge—mostly at the Puritan Emmanuel College—and hence known as the Cambridge Platonists. All of them lived and died within the seventeenth century. The leading representatives of this school were Benjamin Whichcote (1609–83), Ralph Cudworth (1617–88), John Smith (1618–52), and Henry More (1614–87). Although learned, thoughtful, and pious men, loyally devoted to the Church, and animated by a genuine Christian spirit, they were acrimoniously denounced by their opponents, both Anglican and Puritan, as "Rationalists" and "Latitudinarians."

In reply to his Puritan friend, Tuckney, who complained that he gave too great a place to reason and too little importance to faith, Whichcote asserts that "Reason is the very voice of God." "I oppose not rational to spiritual," he says, "for spiritual is most rational." In his view it is only through its appeal that the Gospel can become the principle of our life. Nevertheless he is at pains to point out that the exercise of free judgement must be based on antecedent meditation and prayer. While demanding liberty of conscience, and protesting against the arid dogmatic method prevalent in his time, Whichcote stressed the fundamental truths of all religion, and exercised a powerful influence on contemporary academic thought. Without questioning their piety, the Platonists viewed men like Boehme as "enthusiastic" dreamers carried away by their imagination. Yet they themselves had much in common with Law, one of Boehme's admirers. At the same time, Whichcote and his coadjutors were fitly enough termed Platonists. As diligent students of Plato and Plotinus, they were naturally less attracted to the Dionysian type of thought, but their Platonism was equally remote from a self-centred mystical quietism and from the extravagances of the degenerate Oriental thaumaturgy of the later Neoplatonism. They discussed theological questions from the Platonic standpoint, and asserted the supremacy of reason as the seat of authority in religion. For them a Christian and a rational theology were essentially one. Though not physicists, yet as advocates of a liberal theology they claimed for religion the entire compass of intellectual life. Any real opposition of either philosophy or science to Christian truth was to them unthinkable. The Platonic spirit of Whichcote is revealed in the saying : " Religion is being as much like God as man can be like Him." His appointment in 1644 to the provostship of King's College was in itself an eloquent tribute to his worth, as it is the testimony of Richard Baxter that he was among " the best and ablest of the conformists."

Appended are some extracts from his *Moral and Religious Aphorisms* :

" Knowledge alone doth not amount to virtue ; but certainly there is no virtue without knowledge. Knowledge is the first step to virtue and goodness ; but goodness is not without delight and choice."

" It is a great deal easier to commit a second sin than it was to commit the first, and a great deal harder to repent of a second than it was to repent of the first."

" By these two things religion is recommended to us above all other things whatsoever : (1) By the satisfaction we thereby enjoy in life, and (2) by the expectation we have thereby at death."

" Right and truth are greater than any power, and all power is limited by right."

" Men have an itch : rather to *make* religion than to use it ; but we are to use our religion, not to make it."

" It is the best use of ourselves to be employed about God."

" In the search after God, and contemplation of Him, our wisdom doth consist ; in our worship of God and our obedience to Him our religion doth consist ; in both of them our happiness doth consist."

" He that gives reason for what he saith has done what is fit to be done : he that gives not reason speaks nothing, though he saith never so much."

" To go against reason is to go against God ; it is the self-same thing, to do that which the reason of the case doth require, and that which God Himself doth appoint. Reason is the Divine Governor of man's life ; it is the very voice of God."

" Both Heaven and Hell have their foundation within us.

Heaven primarily lies in a refined temper ; in an internal reconciliation to the nature of God, and to the rule of righteousness. The guilt of conscience, and enmity to righteousness, is the inward state of Hell. The guilt of conscience is the fuel of Hell."

" God hath set up two lights to enlighten us ; the light of Reason, which is the light of His creation, and the light of Scripture, which is after-revelation from Him. Let us make use of these two lights and suffer neither to be put out."

" All is not done when we have spoken to God by prayer ; our petitions are to be pursued with real endeavours ; and our prayers are to be the means and instruments of piety, and virtue must be subservient to a holy life. If they are not the former, they are worth nothing ; if they are not the latter, we but deceive ourselves."

" Regeneration is the salvation of the present state. Glorification is the salvation of the future state."

" We worship God best when we resemble Him most."

" Punishment has in it the notion of a remedy, and has the place of a mean, not of an end. Now as no more of a mean is to be designed than what is necessary to the end ; and a mean is considerable only as it has a relation to the end, there can be no necessity of punishment ; for the end is obtained without it, and there is nothing in punishment save as a mean in which goodness can take content."

" Religion teaches less than we desire to know, and requires more than we are willing to practise."

" In morality we are sure as in mathematics."

" In the Incarnation of Christ we understand God in conjunction with human nature, and this strengthens our faith that human nature may be conjoined to God eternally."

" Christ is God clothed with human nature."

" Christ, who was innocent, was dealt withal as if He were faulty ; that we who are faulty might be dealt withal as if we were innocent."

" The effect of Christ's death in us is our death to sin."

After Whichcote, Ralph Cudworth became leader of the Cambridge Platonists. Without engaging in the controversies between Puritans and Romanists regarding Church government and matters of doctrine, he stoutly defended revealed religion against atheistic and deistic attacks in a huge folio work entitled *The True Intellectual System of the Universe*, and sought to prove the necessity of a moral basis for religion and of human freewill and responsibility. He strongly advocated a happy combination of philosophy and religion. In particular he opposed the materialistic and deterministic arguments of Hobbes as set forth in what Bishop Burnet calls " a very wicked book with a very strange title, *The Leviathan*" (1678). Cudworth's vast, varied, and truly amazing learning, together with his sagacious and eminently prudent conduct, gave him an assured position at the head of the English Platonists, who sought to revive the spirit of the Christian Platonists of Alexandria in the early centuries of our era. His work on *Eternal and Immutable Morality*, from which is taken one of the quotations given below, was not published until after his death. Although in Cudworth the mystical element is less pronounced than the intellectual, he is yet in virtue of his deep-seated Platonism rightly classed as a mystic. Some idea of the character of his writings may be gathered from the following extracts :

" All the knowledge and wisdom that is in creatures, whether angels or men, is nothing else but a participation of that one eternal, immutable, and increated Wisdom of God, or several signatures of that one archetypal seal, or like so many reflections of one and the same Face made in several glasses, whereof some are clearer, some obscurer, some standing near, some farther off.

" Moreover, it was the opinion of the wisest of the philosophers that there is also in the scale of Being a Nature of Goodness superior to Wisdom, which therefore measures and determines the Wisdom of God, as His Wisdom measures and determines His will, and which the ancient Cabalists were wont to call a crown, as being the top or crown of the Deity. Wherefore, although some Novelists make a contracted idea of God, consisting of nothing else but Will and Power ; yet His Nature is better expressed by some in this mystical or enigmatical representation of an infinite circle, whose inmost centre is simple Goodness, the rays and expanded plot thereof, all-comprehending and immutable Wisdom, the exterior periphery or interminate circumference, Omnipotent Will as Activity, by which everything without God is brought forth into existence. Wherefore the will and power of God have no command inwardly either upon the wisdom and knowledge of God, or upon the ethical and moral disposition of His Nature, which is His essential Goodness, but the sphere of its activity is *without God*, where it hath an absolute command upon the Existence of things, and is always free, though not always indifferent, since it is its greatest perfection to be determined by infinite Wisdom and infinite Goodness " (*Eternal and Immutable Morality*, Book i. ch. iii.).

" Because the Atheists look upon Infinity as such a desperate and affrightful thing, we shall here render it something more easy, and take off that frightful vizard from it, which makes it seem such a mormo or bugbear to them ; by declaring in the next place that Infinity is really nothing else but Perfection. For infinite understanding and knowledge is nothing else but perfect knowledge, that which hath no defect or mixture of ignorance with it ; or the knowledge of whatever is knowable. So, in like manner, infinite power is nothing else but perfect power, that which hath no defect or mixture of impotency in it, a power of producing and doing all whatever is possible ; that is, whatsoever is conceivable. Infinite power can do whatsoever infinite understanding can conceive ; conception being the measure of power and its extent, and whatsoever is in itself unconceivable being therefore impossible. Lastly, infinity of duration or eternity is really nothing else but perfection as including necessary existence and immutability in it. So that it is not only contradictions to such a Being to cease to be, or exist ; but also to have had a newness or beginning of being ; or to have any flux or change therein, by dying to the present, and acquiring something new to itself which was not before. Notwithstanding which, this Being comprehends the differences of past, present, and future, or the successive priority and posteriority of all temporary things. And because infinity is perfection, therefore can nothing which includeth anything of imperfection, in the very idea and essence of it, be ever truly and properly infinite, as number, corporeal magnitude, and successive duration. All which can only counterfeit and imitate infinity, in their having more and more added to them *infinitely*, whereby notwithstanding they never reach it or overtake it. There is nothing truly infinite, neither in knowledge, nor in power, nor in duration, but only one absolutely perfect Being or the Holy Trinity" (*The True Intellectual System of the Universe*, Book i. ch. iv. p. 647 f.).

In the constellation of the Cambridge Platonists the next star of the first magnitude was John Smith. He died at the early age of thirty-four, " a thinker without a biography." Like the majority of his associates, he was a graduate of Emmanuel College, and was also elected to a fellowship at Queen's in the same university. His *Select Discourses* (1660), characterized by great erudition and penetrating thought, deal with the immortality of the soul, and the existence and nature of God. It was his intention to include a third section on the communication of God to men through Christ, but he died before this part of his plan was carried out. His Platonism is sufficiently apparent from the declaration that it is only " by a contemplation of our own souls that we can climb up to the understanding of the Deity." He urges that through man's fall from God the vigour of reason has been greatly impaired, "and therefore, besides the truth of natural inscription, God has provided the truth of Divine revelation. . . . But besides this outward revelation there is also an inward impression of it which is in a more formal manner attributed to God. . . . God only can so shine upon our glassy understandings as to beget in them a picture of Himself, and turn the soul like wax or clay to the seal of His own light and love. He that made our souls in His own image and likeness can easily find a way into them. The word that God speaks, having found a way into the soul, imprints itself there as with the point of a diamond. . . . It is God alone that acquaints the soul with the truths of revelation, and also strengthens and raises the soul to better apprehensions even of natural truth, God being that in the intellectual world which the sun is in the sensible, as some of the ancient Fathers love to speak, and the ancient philosophers too, who meant God by their *Intellectus Agens*, whose proper work they supposed to be not so much to enlighten the object as the faculty." [1]

[1] Quoted by W. R. Inge, *op. cit.* p. 289.

Smith's teaching is that only by the light which thus illuminates and purifies the soul can man either rightly understand the things of God or attain the beatific vision for " the sun of truth never shines into any unpurged soul," as is apparent from the words of our Lord : " Blessed are the pure in heart, for they shall see God." In opposition to the *negative way*, he contends that self-denial, properly understood, does not mean the happiness of a hermit or the denying of our own reason, for " that were to deny a beam of the Divine light, and to deny God instead of denying ourselves for Him. . . . It is not a religion to stifle and smother those active powers of principles which are within us." While fully recognizing the delights of the contemplative man's mysterious converses with the Deity, he asserts that the life and knowledge therefrom accruing are " nothing else but an infant-Christ formed in his soul " (see extract below). In this way he sets a limit to ecstatic extravagance. Along with other Platonists, Smith rejects the Calvinistic doctrine of imputed righteousness, and insists on holiness as the *sine qua non* of blessedness. He is at one with Whichcote in regarding heaven and hell not as places but as states of the mind and heart. Very impressive is his spiritual interpretation of the material world. On his reading, the creatures of the universe are mirrors reflecting the Divine glory, the whole creation being a copy of God Himself. To find Him here and to pass out of the sensible world into the intellectual is most effectually taught by true religion, which " doth in a manner spiritualize this outward creation to us." It " beholds itself everywhere in the midst of that glorious unbounded Being who is indivisibly everywhere. A good man finds every place he treads upon holy ground."

Here annexed is a more extended quotation from this writer. Distinguishing a " fourfold kind of knowledge," he says :

" The fourth is the true metaphysical and contemplative man who, running and shooting up above his own logical or self-rational life, pierceth into the highest life : such a one, who by universal love and holy affection abstracteth himself from himself, endeavours the nearest union with the Divine Essence that may be, as Plotinus speaks, knitting his own centre, if he have any, unto the centre of Divine Being. To such an one the Platonists are wont to attribute a true Divine wisdom, powerfully displaying itself in an intellectual life, as they phrase it. Such a knowledge they say is always pregnant with Divine virtue which ariseth out of an happy union of souls with God, and is nothing else but a living imitation of a godlike perfection drawn out by a strong fervent love of it. This Divine knowledge, as Plotinus speaks, makes us amorous of Divine beauty, beautiful and lovely; and this Divine love and purity reciprocally exalts divine knowledge, both of them growing up together like that Ερως and Αντέρως that Pausanias sometimes speaks of. Though by the Platonist's leave such a life and knowledge as this is, peculiarly belongs to the true and sober Christian who lives in Him who is life itself, and is made partaker of the Divine unction, and knoweth all things as St. John speaks. This life is nothing else but God's own breath within him, and an Infant-Christ (if I may use the expression) formed in his soul, who is in a sense the shining forth of the Father's glory. But yet we must not mistake, this knowledge is here but in its infancy; there is an higher knowledge, or an higher degree of this know-ledge that doth not, that cannot, descend upon us in these earthly habitations. We can see here in *speculo lucido*, here we can see *but in a glass*, and that *darkly* too. Our own imaginative powers, which are perpetually attending the highest acts of our souls, will be breathing a gross dew upon the pure glass of our understandings, and so sully and besmear it, that we cannot see the image of the Divinity sincerely in it. But yet this knowledge being a true heavenly fire kindled from God's own altar, begets an undaunted courage in the souls of good men, and enables them to cast an holy scorn upon the poor petty trash of this life in comparison with divine things, and to pity those poor brutish Epicureans that have nothing but the mere husks of fleshly pleasure to feed themselves with. This sight of God makes pious souls breathe after that blessed time when mortality shall be swallowed up of life, when they shall no more behold the Divinity through those dark mediums that eclipse the blessed sight of it " (*The True Way or Method of attaining to Divine Knowledge*, sec. iii.).

The last of the four leading Cambridge Platonists was Henry More, who, after graduating at Christ's College and obtaining a fellowship, remained at the university in the capacity of private tutor. Declining the mastership of his college and also a bishopric, he became in 1675 a prebendary of Gloucester Cathedral. After abandoning Calvinism in favour of theosophy and mysticism, he occupied himself with Kabbalism and various sorts of curious lore. With Glanvil, another of the Platonists, he shared a belief in ghosts and witches, which, says W. S. Tyler, " was a cross between Neoplatonic demonology and modern spiritualism, but whose chief interest to their minds lay in the confirmation it lent to their faith in spiritual existences." More carried his Platonism even to the length of believing in the pre-existence of human souls. But all this was practically without detriment to his steady advance in the spiritual life. To him Christianity was " the deepest and choicest philosophy that is," and holiness the path to knowledge. From the moral nature of man he infers the existence of God, and claims that reason is the judge of the nature of moral goodness, all of which is to be reckoned intellectual and divine. Already in his *Philosophical Poems*, issued in 1647, may be found the germs of his subsequent speculations, and in particular of the tenet that in order rightly to apprehend the Divine it is essential to share in it. Thus he writes :

> But souls that of His own good life partake
>   He loves as His own self : dear as His eye
> They are to Him ; He'll never them forsake :
>   When they shall die, then God Himself shall die :
>   They live, they live in blest eternity.

Burnet speaks of him as " an open-hearted and sincere Christian philosopher, who studied to establish men in the great principles of religion against atheism." At once learned and devoted, modest and hospitable, he exhibited a personality of peculiar charm, and " led the way to many who came after him." Notwithstanding some sympathy with the mystical standpoint, More, like the Platonists in general, strongly emphasized the importance of knowledge and reason, and declared against allegorizing the history of Christ. His was an eminently judicial mind. As Vaughan observes, " he goes a considerable distance with the enthusiast—for he believes that love for the supreme Beautiful and Good may well carry men out of themselves ; but for fanatical presumption he has no mercy."

Subjoined is a brief quotation which may serve as an illustration of his spirit and style :

"I think he need envy nobody who has his heart full fraught with the love of God, and his mind established in a firm belief of that unspeakable happiness that the virtuous or pious soul enjoys in the other state amongst ' the spirits of just men made perfect.' The firm belief of this in an innocent soul is so high a prelibation of those eternal joys, that it equalizes such an one's happiness, if he have but the ordinary conveniences of life, to that of the greatest potentates. Their difference in external fortune is as little considerable as a semidiameter of the earth in two measures of the highest heaven ; the one taken from the surface of the earth, the other from its centre : the disproportion you know is just nothing" (*Divine Dialogues*).

Principal Tulloch (*Rational Theology*, 1874) summarily distinguishes the four leaders of the Cambridge Platonists thus : " Benjamin Whichcote, reason and religion ; John Smith, foundations of a Christian philosophy ; Ralph Cudworth, Christian philosophy in conflict with materialism ; Henry More, Christian philosophy and mysticism."

Among other noted adherents of the Platonists were : (1) John Wilkins (1614–72), who studied at Oxford, but went to join the new school of liberal theologians at Cambridge, where he became Master of Trinity. An expert in both natural and mental philosophy, " he was a lover of mankind, and had a delight in doing good." In 1668 he was made bishop of Chester. (2) Dr. Worthington, who edited Smith's *Discourses*, and of whom Burnet says he was " a man of eminent piety, of great humility, and practised a most sublime way of self-denial and devotion." (3) John Tillotson (1630–94), a man with the best qualities of head and heart, and widely honoured and beloved as the foremost preacher of his time. His sermons are marked by fertility of thought, but are rather lacking in literary grace. Contrary to his own wishes he was appointed Archbishop of Canterbury, and in his later days suffered much from the fierce attacks of the non-jurors. (4) Edward Stillingfleet (1635–99), whose learning exceeded that of Tillotson. In 1659 was published his *Irenicum*, a masterly treatise on Church government, in which, with a catholicity of spirit remarkable at that period of ecclesiastical strife, he put forward the view that the apostles had left it an open question. In 1689 he became Bishop of Worcester. Besides writing copiously on Biblical or theological themes, Stillingfleet was an ardent champion of Protestantism. As a metaphysician, too, his calibre may be judged from his repeated criticisms of Locke's famous *Essay*. His sermons have been praised for their " good sense and force of style."

Bishop Burnet remarks on the service rendered by those men in bringing about a reform in the method of preaching. Their style, he says, was " clear, plain, and short," and not, as had been previously the case among Church divines, " overrun with pedantry." And to this may be added the general estimate formed by Dr. Inge : " The English Platonists breathe a larger air than the later Romish mystics, and teach a religion more definitely Christian than Erigena and Eckhart."

(2) *William Law*

We have next to take account of William Law (1686–1761), non-juror, controversialist, devotional writer, and mystic. On completing his studies and gaining a fellowship at Emmanuel College, Cambridge, he took orders in 1711, but seems to have been mainly engaged in teaching until the accession of George I. in 1714, when his refusal to take the oath of allegiance deprived him both of his fellowship and of all hope of ecclesiastical promotion. About the age of forty he was appointed private tutor to Edward Gibbon, father of the famous historian, and for some years accompanied his pupil to Cambridge. Subsequently at Putney he acted as the valued friend and adviser of the Gibbon family, and became closely associated with the brothers Wesley, and with the stenographer and poet John Byrom, whose entertaining *Journal* contains not a few illuminating touches with respect to himself. By the death of the elder Gibbon in 1732 these relations

were dislocated, and Law returned to his birthplace at
King's Cliffe, Northamptonshire, as heir to a small paternal
property. Thither he was accompanied by Hester Gibbon,
aunt of the historian, and Mrs. Hutcheson, the widow of a
friend of his own, both being ladies of independent means.
Pooling their resources, all three devoted themselves to the
cultivation of piety and the practice of benevolence. An
unexpected anonymous gift of a thousand pounds, the
grateful offering of some one who had profited by Law's
earlier writings, had enabled him to found a residential
school for a number of poor girls ; and now, aided by the
co-operation of his two like-minded associates, and probably by royalties from the sale of his books, schools were
established for orphans and quarters for widows, as well
as houses for schoolmasters, and a library, still known as
The Law and Hutcheson Charities. Among other rules it
was provided in the constitution of these foundations that
the Rector of King's College for the time being is always
to be a trustee, and that the children are to be constant at
church at all times of Divine service, as well on week-days
as on Sundays.

In an age of rationalistic thought Law was a powerful
advocate of evangelical religion. " To come across such a
man in the midst of his surroundings," says his biographer
Overton, " is like coming a cross an old Gothic cathedral,
with its air of calm grandeur and mellowed beauty, in the
midst of the staring red-brick buildings of a brand-new
manufacturing town." His *Three Letters* in reply to a
sermon preached in 1717 before King George I. by Dr.
Hoadly, Bishop of Bangor, on *The Nature of the Kingdom
of the Church of Christ*, and published by authority of the
Court, shewed him to be a sturdy controversialist, and the
High Church party as well as the non-jurors of those days
hailed with delight his doughty defence against the censures
of the free-thinking bishop.

Law was an excellent writer. His clear style, logical
reasoning, practical standpoint, and elevation of mind,
place him in the front line of the literary men of his time,
while as a devotional writer he has admittedly few equals.
His numerous works are entitled to rank as religious classics.
Specially is this true of his *Treatise on Christian Perfection*
(1726) and his *Serious Call to a Devout and Holy Life* (1729).

In both of these he deals in a searching and masterly way with the vital matter of personal religion. To read his book on Christian perfection is to see with what unerring skill he leads the soul out of the depths of fallen human nature to the heights of Christian experience, where every thought is brought into captivity to the obedience of Christ. It is, however, by his *Serious Call* that Law is best known. This is a work of singular power, and, as stated in the preface to one of its many editions, " with the exception of the *Pilgrim's Progress* there is no religious book in the English language which has had a stronger influence." Judges of the first order vie with each other in extolling its excellence. According to Dr. Johnson, it is " the finest piece of hortatory theology in any language." Augustine Birrell speaks of " the inimitable author," and says that even Gibbon's *Decline and Fall* is " a poor and barren thing compared with the *Serious Call*, which has proved its power to pierce the heart and tame the will." It is interesting to know that Gibbon himself appreciated its merits. " Law's masterpiece," he writes, " is a powerful book. His precepts are rigid, but they are founded on the Gospel : his satire is sharp, but it is drawn from his knowledge of human life, and many of his portraits are not unworthy the pen of La Bruyère." In his riper years John Wesley, too, describes it as " a treatise which will hardly be excelled, if it be equalled, in the English tongue, either for beauty of expression or for justness and depth of thought." This is a testimony of peculiar value as coming from one who, after having looked upon Law as " a kind of oracle," had for long been in sharp opposition to him, partly because of doctrinal differences, and partly because of " the false censure which he published against the mystics." The unhappy antagonism between these two great and good men is reflected in Wesley's *Journal*. As thus : " I read over Mr. Law's book on the New Birth : philosophical, speculative, precarious ; Behemenish, void and vain." Again : " I read Mr. Law on the Spirit of Prayer. There are many masterly strokes therein, and the whole is lively and entertaining ; but it is another Gospel : for if God was never angry (as this Tract asserts) He could never be reconciled ; and consequently the whole Christian doctrine of Reconciliation by Christ falls to the ground at once.

8

An excellent method of converting Deists ! by giving up the very essence of Christianity." Dr. Alexander Whyte suggestively remarks that " Law and Wesley in their intellectual life and their religious experience, as well as in the work to which their Master had called them, were perhaps as different as two able and good men could well be. Wesley was fitted to be a popular and most impressive preacher, while Law was never allowed to preach, but was early set apart by Divine Providence to think and read and write. . . . And surely, if they could only both have seen it, there was scope enough and call enough within the limits of Evangelical Christianity for two such signally gifted if signally individual men. . . . Could they both have seen it, both were indispensable : John Wesley to complete William Law, and William Law to complete John Wesley."

The following is an extract from the opening chapter of the *Serious Call* : " Devotion signifies a life given, or devoted, to God. He, therefore, is the devout man, who lives no longer to his own will, or the way and spirit of the world, but to the sole will of God ; who considers God in everything, who serves God in everything, who makes all the parts of his common life parts of piety, by doing everything in the Name of God, and under such rules as are conformable to His glory. We readily acknowledge that God alone is to be the rule and measure of our prayers ; that in them we are to look wholly unto Him and act wholly for Him ; that we are only to pray in such a manner, for such things, and such ends, as are suitable to His glory.

Now let any one but find out the reason why he is to be thus strictly pious in his prayers, and he will find the same as strong a reason to be as strictly pious in all the other parts of his life. For there is not the least shadow of a reason why we should make God the rule and measure of our prayers ; why we should then look wholly unto Him, and pray according to His will ; but what equally proves it necessary for us to look wholly unto God, and make Him the rule and measure of all the other actions of our life. For any ways of life, any employment of our talents, whether of our parts, our time, or money, that is not strictly according to the will of God, that is not for such ends as are suitable to His glory, are as great absurdities and failings as prayers that are not according to the will of God. For there is no other reason why our prayers should be according to the will of God, why they should have nothing in them but what is wise, and holy, and heavenly; there is no other reason for this, but that our lives may be of the same nature, full of the same wisdom, holiness, and heavenly tempers, that we may live unto God in the same spirit that we pray unto Him. Were it not our strict duty to live by reason, to devote all the actions of our lives to God, were it not absolutely necessary to walk before Him in wisdom and holiness and all heavenly conversation, doing everything in His name, and for His glory, there would be no excellency or wisdom in the most heavenly prayers. Nay, such prayers would be absurdities; they would be like prayers for wings, when it was no part of our duty to fly.

"As sure, therefore, as there is any wisdom in praying for the Spirit of God, so sure is it that we are to make that spirit the rule of all our actions; as sure as it is our duty to look wholly unto God in our prayers, so sure is it that it is our duty to live wholly unto God in our lives. But we can no more be said to live unto God, unless we live unto Him in all the ordinary actions of our life, unless He be the rule and measure of all our ways, than we can be said to pray unto God, unless our prayers look wholly unto Him. So that unreasonable and absurd ways of life, whether in labour or diversion, whether they consume our time or our money, are like unreasonable and absurd prayers, and are as truly an offence unto God."

The year 1734 witnessed a new and important development in Law's thought and writings. It was then that he came under the spell of Jacob Boehme, and began to infuse into his own works the mysticism of that writer. Even before he was acquainted with the writings of Boehme, however, the mystic strain which latterly became so pronounced in him, is clearly traceable. Deeply engraven on his heart are the words of Jesus: "The kingdom of God is within you." He is also keenly alive to the declaration of St. Paul: "The invisible things of God are clearly seen from the creation of the world, being understood by the things that are made" (Ro 1[20]), "so that the outward condition and frame of visible nature is a plain manifestation of that spiritual world from which it is descended." One does not need to read far into his works in order to discover the validity of his claim to have been " a diligent reader of the mystical divines through all ages of the Church." Thus he says : " To find or know God in reality by any outward proofs or by anything but by God Himself made manifest and self-evident in you, will never be your case either here or hereafter " (*The Way to Divine Knowledge*).

And again : " Self is an inward life, and God is an Inward Spirit of Life ; therefore, nothing kills that which must be killed in us, or quickens that which must come to life in us, but the inward work of God in the soul, and the inward work of the soul in God. This is that mystic religion which, though it has nothing in it but that same spirit, that same truth, and that same life, which always was, and always must be the religion of all God's holy angels and saints in heaven, is by the wisdom of this world accounted to be madness " (*An Humble Address to the Clergy*). Boehme's mystical influence is particularly apparent in the Tract upon the *Grounds and Reasons of Christian Regeneration* (1739), and in the two works in which he replies to objections against his views, namely, *The Spirit of Prayer* (1749) and *The Spirit of Love* (1752). A few extracts will convey the nature of their teaching better than any comments can.

On Christian Regeneration he writes as follows : " It is to be observed that regeneration, or the renewal of our first birth and state, is something entirely distinct from this first sudden conversion or call to repentance ; that it is not a thing done in an instant, but it is a certain process, a gradual release from our captivity and disorder, consisting of several stages and degrees, both of death and life, which the soul must go through before it can have thoroughly put off the old man. I will not say that this must needs be in the same degree in all, or that there cannot be any exception to this. But thus much is true and certain, that Jesus Christ is our Pattern, that what He did for us that we are also to do for ourselves, or, in other words, we must follow Him in the regeneration." Further, " He is a true Christian who, as our blessed Lord speaks, has the kingdom of God within him, where the state and habit

of his heart continually, thankfully, worships the Father
in spirit and in truth."

Subjoined are some selections from *The Spirit of Prayer*.
Regarding God, Nature, and Creatures, he says : "Nature
itself is a birth from God ; it is the first manifestation of
the hidden inconceivable God, and it is so far from being
out of nothing that it is the manifestation of all that in
God which was before unmanifest. As nature is the
first birth or manifestation of God or discovery of the
Divine powers, so all creatures are the manifestation of
the powers of nature brought into a variety of births by
the will of God out of nature. The first creatures that are
the nearest to the Deity are out of the highest powers of
nature, God willing that nature should be manifested in
the rise and birth of creatures out of it. Nature, directed
and governed by the Wisdom of God, goes on in the birth
of one thing out of another." Evil he describes as "nothing
else but the wrath, and fire, and darkness of nature broken
off from God ; the punishment, the pain, or the hell of
sin, is no designedly prepared or arbitrary penalty inflicted
by God, but the natural and necessary state of the creature
that leaves or turns from God" (*An Appeal*, etc., p. 28).

Of Christ he speaks thus : "He is the universal Remedy
of all evil broken forth in nature and creature. He is
the Destruction of misery, sin, darkness, death, and
hell. He is the Resurrection and Life of all fallen nature.
He is the unwearied Compassion, the long-suffering Pity,
the never-ceasing Mercifulness of God to every want and
infirmity of human nature. He is the Breathing forth of
the heart, life, and spirit of God into all the dead race of
Adam. He is the Seeker, the Finder, the Restorer of all
that was lost and dead to the life of God. He is the Love
that from Cain to the end of time prays for all its murderers ;
the Love that willingly suffers and dies among thieves that
thieves may have a life with Him in Paradise ; the Love
that visits publicans, harlots, and sinners, and wants and
seeks to forgive where most is to be forgiven" (*The Spirit
of Prayer*, ii. p. 127.)

Concerning the Cross, he writes : "The doctrine of the
Cross of Christ, the last, the highest, the most finishing
stroke given to the spirit of this world, that speaks more in
one word than all the philosophy of voluminous writers,

is yet professed by those who are in more friendship with the world than was allowed to the disciples of Pythagoras, Socrates, Plato, or Epictetus. Nay, if those ancient sages were to start up among us with their Divine wisdom, they would bid fair to be treated by the sons of the gospel, if not by some fathers of the Church as dreaming enthusiasts." (*The Spirit of Prayer*, ii. pp. 105, 115.)

Dealing with the mystery of the Atonement, Law says : " When it is by the letter of Scripture revealed to us that the blessed Jesus is the One Mediator between God and men ; that He is the Atonement, the Propitiation, and Satisfaction for our sins : these expressions only teach us as much outward knowledge of so great a mystery as human language can represent. For that, being a Divine and supernatural matter, cannot by any outward words be revealed to us, any more than the Essence of God can be made visible to our eyes of flesh " (*The Case of Reason*, p. 39).

Of the New Life he remarks : " All our salvation consists in the manifestation of the Nature, Life, and Spirit of Jesus Christ in our inward new man. This alone is Christian redemption, this alone delivers from the guilt and power of sin, this alone redeems, renews, and regains the first life of God in the soul of man. Everything besides this is self, is fiction, is propriety, is own will, and, however coloured, is only thy old man, with all his deeds. . . . From morning to night keep Jesus in thy heart, long for nothing, desire nothing, hope for nothing, but to have all that is within thee changed into the spirit and temper of the Holy Jesus. Let this be thy Christianity, thy church, and thy religion" (*The Spirit of Prayer*, p. 49).

" Prayer," he urges, " cannot be taught you by giving you a book of prayers, but by awakening in you a true sense and knowledge of what you are and what you should be ; that so you may see and know and feel what things you want and are to pray for. For a man does not, cannot, pray for anything because a fine petition for it is put into his hands, but because his own condition is a reason and motive for his asking for it " (*The Spirit of Prayer*, p. 176).

From *The Spirit of Love* we quote as follows : " What an eternity is this, out of which and for which thy eternal soul was created ! What little crawling things are all

that an earthly ambition can set before thee ! Bear with
patience for a while the rags of thy earthly nature, the
veil and darkness of flesh and blood, as the lot of thy
inheritance from father Adam, but think nothing worth a
thought but that which will bring thee back to thy first
glory and land thee safe in the region of eternity." Again :
" Divine Love is perfect Peace and Joy, it is a freedom
from all disquiet, it is all content and mere happiness, and
makes everything to rejoice in itself. Love is the Christ
of God ; wherever it comes, it comes as the blessing and
happiness of every natural life, as the Restorer of every
lost perfection, a Redeemer from all evil, a Fulfiller of all
righteousness, and a Peace of God which passeth all understanding. Through all the universe of things, nothing is
uneasy, unsatisfied, or restless, but because it is not
governed by love, or because its nature has not reached or
attained the full birth of the Spirit of Love. For when
that is done, every hunger is satisfied, and all complaining,
murmuring, accusing, resenting, revenging, and striving,
are as totally suppressed and overcome as the coldness,
thickness, and horror of darkness are suppressed and overcome by the breaking forth of the light."

Law's theology is emphatically that of the heart. In *The
Spirit of Love*, following up the declaration (in *The Spirit
of Prayer*) that " your heart alone has the key of life and
death," he says : " What a folly, then, to be so often
perplexed about the way to God ! For nothing is the way
to God but our heart. God is nowhere else to be found,
and the heart itself cannot find Him, or be helped by
anything else to find Him, but by its own love of Him,
faith in Him, dependence upon Him, resignation to Him,
and expectation of all from Him."

Doctrinally, it will be observed that the Law's view of
the Atonement coincides with that of Boehme. He
strongly opposes the forensic theory, and insists that
" Christ given for us is neither more nor less than Christ
given into us. He is in no sense our full, perfect, and
sufficient Atonement than as His nature and spirit are born
and formed in us." Nor is he less positive in declaring
that the Cross is no reflection of the Divine wrath, but only
of infinite Love. Wrath, he holds, is dissolved by the
extinction of sin. " I know of no hell, either here or here-

after, but the power and working of wrath, nor any heaven but where the God of love is all in all " (*The Spirit of Love*). Heaven is thus everywhere.

Regarding free will he writes: " The will is not a made thing, or a thing that came out of some different state into the state of a will. But the free will of man is a true and real birth from the free, eternal, uncreated will of God, which willed to have a creaturely offspring of itself, or to see itself in a creaturely state. And therefore the will of man hath the nature of Divine freedom; hath the nature of eternity, and the nature of Omnipotence in it, because it is what it is, and hath what it hath, as a spark, a ray, a genuine birth of the eternal, free, omnipotent will of God" (*The Way to Divine Knowledge*).

Law lays great stress on the duty of intercessory prayer. " Our Blessed Lord hath recommended His love to us as the pattern and example of our love to one another. As therefore He is continually making intercession for us all, so ought we to intercede and pray for one another. . . . Intercession is not only the best arbitrator of all differences, the best promoter of true friendship, the best cure and preservative against all unkind tempers, all angry and haughty passions, but is also of great use to discover to us the true state of our own hearts " (*Serious Call*, ch. xxi.).

In his *Christian Perfection* Law gives us his estimate of Learning. " If you can shew me a learning that makes man truly sensible of his duty, that fills the mind with true light, that reforms the heart, that disposes it right towards God, that makes us more reasonable in all our actions, that inspires us with fortitude, humility, devotion, and contempt of the world, that gives us right notions of the greatness of religion, the sanctity of morality, the littleness of everything but God, the vanity of our passions, and the misery and corruption of our nature, I will own myself an advocate for such learning. But to think that time is well employed because it is spent in such speculations as the vulgar cannot reach, or because they are fetched from antiquity, or found in Greek or Latin, is a folly that may be called as great as any in human life."

Corresponding to Law's eminence as a thinker and a writer was the strength and beauty of his character. It is the fine eulogium of Gibbon that he "believed all that he professed, and practised all that he enjoined." On 9th April 1761 this truly saintly man entered into his everlasting rest.

To conclude : it seems appropriate to advert to Law's statements concerning his attitude towards "God's illuminated Boehme." These, it will be seen, are uniformly of the most admiring and respectful character. If in any respect Law parts company with Boehme, it is in the matter of careful adherence to the ordinances of the Church. While not overestimating outward observances, and while setting the highest value on the inward worship of the soul, so that "wherever thou goest thou wilt have a priest, a church and an altar along with thee," he scrupulously observed the ordinances of the Church in whose communion he had been reared. It may also be noted that, though an enthusiastic admirer of Jacob Boehme, Law avoided the wild extravagances of some of that theosophist's disciples.

In *An Appeal to all that Doubt* (1740), Law writes : "Jacob Boehme, in his natural capacity and outward condition of life, was as mean and illiterate as any one that our Lord called to be an apostle, but as a chosen servant of God he may be placed among those who had received the highest measures of light, wisdom, and knowledge from above. He was no more a human writer, spoke no more from opinion, conjecture, or reason, in what he published to the world, than St. John did, when he put his Revelation into writing. He has no right to be placed among the inspired penmen of the New Testament ; he was no messenger from God in anything new in religion ; but the mystery of all that was old and true, both in religion and nature, was opened in him. This is the particularity of his character, by which he stands fully distinguished from all the prophets, apostles, and extraordinary messengers of God."

In a *Letter to a Clergyman* (1753) he says : "All that I have wrote for near thirty years has been only to shew that we have no Master but Christ, nor can have any living Divine knowledge but from His Holy Nature born and revealed in us. Not a word in favour of Jacob Behmen, but because, above every writer in the world, he has made all that is found in the kingdom of grace and the kingdom of nature to be one continued demonstration that, dying to self, to be born again of Christ, is the only possible salvation of the sons of fallen Adam."

Then we find him writing in 1757 to Dr. Sherlock : " I am conscious that in my later writings I have raised a prejudice against me by espousing the writings of Jacob Behmen.   It was very easy for the world to find fault with me on that account.   Matter of censure lies very open to the critical reader of his books, though the true ground of every doctrine and article of Christian faith is there opened in such a ravishing, amazing depth, and clearness of truth and conviction, as had never been seen or thought of in any age of the Church."

Finally, there are his references to Sir Isaac Newton's obligations to Boehme.   In *An Appeal*, etc., he expresses his conviction that the author of *The Principia* owed the groundwork of his teaching on gravitation and the laws regulating the motions of the planets in their orbits to the " Teutonic Theosopher," and was prevented from saying so only because the new doctrines would have been seriously prejudiced if in any way associated with " an author who was only called an enthusiast."   Similarly, in his *Spirit of Love*, he observes : " Here also, that is, in these three properties of the desire, you see the ground and reason of the three great laws of matter and motion lately discovered and so much celebrated, and need no more to be told that the illustrious Sir Isaac Newton ploughed with Behmen's heifer when he brought forth the discovery of them."

PART IV

THE BASIC PRINCIPLES AND MAIN FEATURES OF CHRISTIAN MYSTICISM

HERE we purposely leave on one side many features of Mysticism more or less associated with its manifest types, taking no account, for example, of Symbolism and Allegorism, of the generally recognized stages and subdivisions of the spiritual life, or of the extreme asceticisms so zealously affected by certain of its votaries. Our concern is simply with the essential principles and main features of Christian Mysticism. Can they be definitely stated?

The following chief points, at least, may reasonably be specified:

I. A keen sense of the spiritual as the truly real, or "the urge which makes us realize the inner meaning of life."—The Christian mystic is an idealist. He regards himself as, in the words of the author of *John Inglesant*, "an immortal spirit walking among supernatural things— for the natural things of this life would be nothing were they not moved and animated by the efficacy of that which is above nature." This is the first and broader of the two basic principles of Christian Mysticism, and holds good in the case of all to whom the term may justifiably be applied. It is theirs to say with St. Paul: "Now we have received the Spirit—not the spirit of the world, but the spirit that comes from God, that we may understand the things that are freely given to us by God" (1 Co 2[12]). Such spiritual sensibility leads to what must rank as the second and more particular root of Christian Mysticism, namely:

II. Self-renunciation.—While on the part of every Christian worthy of the name there is implied a yielding up of himself, body, soul, and spirit, unto God (Ro 6[20];

cf. 1 Thess 5²³), this is peculiarly exemplified in the mystic. None can claim more truly than he to have adopted the attitude of the Apostle : "Wherever I go I am being killed in the body as Jesus was, so that the life of Jesus may come out in my body : Every day of my life I am being given over to death for Jesus' sake, so that the life of Jesus may come out within my mortal flesh" (2 Co 4¹⁰ᶠ·). That is to say, he dies to live—a deftly paradoxical statement of the mystic's mental attitude towards religion. Of this perfect self-renunciation there is perhaps no finer modern expression than that contained in Miss Havergal's familiar hymn from its opening lines :

> Take my life, and let it be
> Consecrated, Lord, to Thee,

to those with which it ends :

> Take myself, and I will be
> Ever, only, all for Thee!

Such, in brief, is the twofold groundwork on which Christian Mysticism essentially rests. Its distinctive features call for somewhat more extended notice. They are mainly these :

(1) Contemplation.—The word has both a general and a special meaning. Viewed generally, it signifies continued concentration of the mind on any particular subject. More specifically it denotes deep attention to things sacred, as when it is said :

> I have toward heaven breathed a secret vow
> To live in prayer and contemplation. ¹

This is the distinctive meaning of the term as marking a leading feature of mystical religion. Prayerful meditation is indispensably preparatory to the contemplative life.

Notably such a life has both its pleasures and its dangers. When Tennyson speaks of

> Falling into a still delight
> And luxury of contemplation,²

he is not using the word in a religious sense, though his

---

¹ Shakespeare, *Merchant of Venice*, Act III.
² " Eleänora," l. 51.

language might quite well be so applied. That such contemplation has certainly its delights is axiomatically assumed by our great dramatist as he further writes :

> When holy and devout religious men
> Are at their beads, 'tis hard to draw them thence,
> So sweet is zealous contemplation. [1]

Abundant evidence of this occurs even in the autobiography and letters of so practically minded a mystic as St. Teresa. Concerning the delights of prayer she remarks : " The joys of prayer should be somewhat like those others which are in heaven." [2] Writing to Father Gratian, she says, however, " That prayer is the most acceptable which leaves the best results. Results, I mean, in actions. Not certain gusts of softness and feeling, but that which improves me in virtue." Again she observes : " Mental prayer becomes conjoined with vocal . . . whence it falls out that those who pray vocally are often by God exalted, without perceiving it themselves, to *Contemplation*," [3] so that in her view prayer produces the best effects alike in the sphere of active virtue and in that of mystic contemplation.

But if contemplation be a luxury, it can also be a peril. Another of our great poets indicates its dangers. Referring to what he elsewhere calls " the Cherub Contemplation," [4] Milton in *Paradise Lost* draws this picture :

> Others apart sat on a hill retired,
> In thoughts more elevate, and reasoned high
> Of providence, foreknowledge, will, and fate,
> Fixed fate, free will, forethought absolute,
> And found no end, in wandering mazes lost. [5]

In its most specific mystical sense contemplation denotes ecstatic rapture—a shortlived experience, a moment of insight, in which the soul enjoys immediate contact with God, and which, though it is but transient, has an abiding influence upon the life of him or her to whom it is vouchsafed. Not, however, that such perfect contemplation or " supernatural prayer " is without its dangers—dangers exceeding even those of the inextricable metaphysical labyrinths poetically envisaged by Milton, and besetting many who never attained to ecstasy. According to

---

[1] *Richard III.*, Act III. sc. 7.   [2] *Life*, ch. x.
[3] *Ibid.* ch. xxxvi.   [4] *Il Penseroso*, l. 51.   [5] Book ii., l. 555 ff

Coventry Patmore,[1] the dangers confronting contemplative mysticism are chiefly these : (1) It tends to make the soul insatiably hunger for more such seasons of revelation, and to render it in a greater or less degree impervious to the prophetic injunction. "Though the vision tarry, wait for it " (Hab 2³). Love can always wait. (2) Ecstatic rapture is also subject to the temptation to be disobedient to the heavenly vision and to become slack in point of moral discipline. (3) For the rest, the seer is only too apt to make the mistake of supposing that what he has only *seen* has become his in actual possession.

If, then, contemplation be an essential element of Christian Mysticism, and if on the one hand it is capable of yielding superlative joys, and on the other of leading to devious and perilous paths, what general estimate is to be put upon it ? How is its value to be appraised ?

It has sometimes been represented as consisting in mere sentimental absorption in the Absolute. This, however, is a wrong conception, based principally upon the vagaries of mystical sectaries belonging for the most part to the Beghards and Brethren of the Free Spirit. It is contradicted not merely by the often cited example of St. Catherine of Genoa, whose mystical sense never interfered with her faithful efficiency as a nurse, but by many other parallel instances as well. Moreover, it is repudiated by all the great mystics themselves. These have nothing too hard to say of a mysticism that is simply emotional and non-moral. Ruysbroek, Teresa, Boehme, and many others, insist upon active fruitfulness in good works, and upon positive holiness and disciplined piety as well as upon contemplation. They see no incongruity, and acknowledge no divorce between the active and the contemplative religious life. They would have acclaimed the judicial statement of Baron von Hügel relative to the proper balance between the two. "What is wanted," says this learned author, "if we would really cover the facts of the case, is evidently not a conception which would minimize the human action and would represent the latter as shrinking in proportion as God's action increases ; but one which, on the contrary, fully faces,

[1] The Rod, the Root, and the Flower : *Aurea Dicta*, cxi. ; *Magna Moralia*, xx. (quoted by E. Herman).

and keeps a firm hold of, the mysterious paradox which pervades all true life, and which shews us the human soul as self active in proportion to God's action within it. . . . Grace and the Will thus rise and fall, in their degree of action, together ; and man will never be so fully active, so truly and intensely himself, as when he is most truly possessed by God."[1] Yet the practical activities of the mystics must not be too strongly stressed. If they were not mere passive dreamers, neither were they eminently practical. Their heart was set not upon work, but upon union with the Unseen in the inmost depths of their souls. After all, they valued good works only in so far as these formed a stepping-stone to this as their ultimate goal. Everything was subordinated to the idea of entire devotion to God. Prayer and inward contemplation they deemed to be of more spiritual value than either church extension or deeds of charity. Throughout the centuries their ruling principle has been : " Be still, and know that I am God " (Ps. 46[10]). Not that such stillness is to be reckoned as mere idleness. On the contrary, it implies an eager receptivity in which every faculty of the soul is keenly alert. It is the listening attitude of the child Samuel saying : " Speak, Lord, for Thy servant heareth," the presupposition being that it is only to the quietly listening soul that the King of Love and Glory will come in. By this means it is hoped to arrive at the knowledge of God. Nor is the soul's active yearning after God neutralized by this passive waiting for Him. In the mystic life the one factor is not cancelled by the other. To quote Mrs. Herman : " Both have a place in the spiritual life ; but in the Orison of Quiet it is the passive and not the active side that (though the latter is present also) gives its character to the whole. Passivity is an essential element in all genuine religion. . . . " It is here," she characteristically and pithily adds, " that the message of mystic Quiet lies for a garrulous and facile generation."[2]

(2) "The Process of Christ" in us.—The phrase is a favourite one of William Law's, and may perhaps be taken to express the point of view of Mysticism in general, according to which in the ordinary conception of the work of redemption too exclusive emphasis is laid upon

[1] *The Mystical Element of Religion*, i. p. 80.   [2] *Op. cit.* p. 121 f.

Christ's work *for* us, to the virtual neglect of the vital factor of His work *in* us. While all the mystics insist on the importance of the Master's declaration, " The kingdom of God is within you," William Law may be said to have given this principle its fullest development. Arguing that " if man was to go out of his fallen state, there must be a son of this fallen man, who, as head and fountain of the whole race, could go back through all the gates closed by the Fall," and, opening them one by one, clear for " all individual members of human nature, as being born of him," the way to eternal life. Now, contends the " non-juror and mystic," this is what the Second Adam has done. The gospel shews us Christ Jesus " entering in and going through all the parts of this process." These include " His personality, His birth, His life, His sufferings, His death, His resurrection, and ascension into heaven." This is the great mystery, " kept secret since the world began," until fully revealed in His actual appearance. The first gate was opened when Jesus became flesh. The second stage in His " whole process " was that of life without spot. Following upon this was the crucial stage of His last sufferings and death upon the cross, in which He made a sacrificial offering of Himself to God and bore away the sin of the world. As the Second Adam He " entered into the real horrors of that eternal death, which man unredeemed must have died into when he left this world." This experienced, He could triumphantly say, " It is finished." He could not be holden of death, and on the third day rose again " according to the Scriptures." Thereby He opened the gateway into Paradise, thus abolishing death and bringing life and immortality to light. This was the penultimate stage in His great " process." It remained only that He should ascend into heaven and occupy His place as our Advocate and Intercessor at the right hand of the Majesty on high. Such in brief is Law's teaching with respect to " the one whole process of Christ." [1] Its significance for us, however, is in his judgement not exhausted by the contemplation of its several component parts and progressive stages. Religion is a way of life, and the way of the Christian is the

[1] See *An Appeal to all that Doubt*, p. 190 ff., and *A Short but Sufficient Confutation*, etc., pp. 12, 94.

way of Christ. This means that we must follow Him in the various stages of His progress, and overcome sin by renewing in our own lives the experiences which He underwent. We must be reborn and become new creatures in Him. Thereafter in our daily life we must take Him for our pattern and follow His steps. Suffering will be our portion as it was His. With Him, too, we must be crucified and die ; but knowing the fellowship of His sufferings, we shall also know the power of His resurrection. Moreover, it is His assurance that those whom the Father has given Him shall ascend and be with Him, that they may behold His glory, and share in the benefits of His eternal priesthood. All these are essential links in the chain of His marvellous " process," and in their combination restore to human nature in its fulness what it lost by the Fall. This stupendous result is wholly due to the personality and power of Christ. By the inspiration of His Spirit He also enables His disciples to take up their cross and follow Him till they enter through the open gates into the eternal city. Such in its nature and implications—if we may accept William Law as spokesman for the mystical fraternity as a whole—is " the wonderful process of Christ."

3. Yearning for union with God.—To this all Christian mystics eagerly aspire, but as to the nature of this union we meet with no uniform conception. Not only so ; prominent representatives of the mystical tendency are not always consistent with themselves in their teaching. This peculiarly holds good, for example, even of the famous Meister Eckhart. At one time he says : " We should be united in God essentially, we should be united in God individually, we should be united in God entirely. How should we be united in God essentially ? This must be done in contemplation and not substantially. His substance cannot become our substance, though it must be our life." At another time he says : " We shall become the same essence and substance and nature that He is himself, without any difference." [1] Thus the clear distinction drawn in the first statement is wholly obliterated by the metaphysical pantheism of the second. More helpful is it to turn to St. Teresa when she speaks of God

[1] For these and further quotations see Gieseler, *Ecclesiastical History*, iv. p. 178, English translation.

within the soul. " It is an ennobling thing," she says,
" to think that God is more in the soul of man than He is
in aught else outside of Himself. They are happy people
who have once got hold of this glorious truth. In particular,
the Blessed Augustine testifies that neither in the home
nor in the church, nor anywhere else, did he find God, till
once he had found Him in himself. Nor had he need to
go up to heaven, but only down into himself to find God "
(*Life*, ch. xxxvi.). Again she says : " In prayer there
would sometimes come upon one such a sense of the
Presence of God that I seemed to be all engulfed in God.
I think the learned call this mystical experience ; at any
rate it so suspends the ordinary operations of the soul
that she seems to be wholly taken out of herself. This
tenderness, this sweetness, this regale, is nothing but the
Presence of God in the praying soul " (*Life*, ch. x.). And
again (in *The Interior Castle*) : " Let us suppose ' union '
to be like two tapers, so exactly joined together that the
light of both makes but one ; or that the wick, light, and
wax, are all one and the same, but that, afterwards, one
taper may be easily divided from the other, and then two
distinct tapers will remain and the wick will be distinct
from the wax. But here (in the spiritual espousals) it is
like water descending from heaven into a river or spring,
where one is so mixed with the other, that it cannot be
discovered which is the river-water and which is the rain.
. . . This is perhaps that which St. Paul means when he
says : ' He who adheres to God is one with Him.' " [1]
More specifically she states that this union consists in the
conformity of our will to God's (*Foundations*, ch. x.).
Once more, regarding the union of the soul with God, she
writes : " You see that God makes this soul quite stupid,
she neither sees, nor heeds, nor understands, nor perceives
in order to imprint the deeper in her true wisdom ; hence
all the time she is in this state, and this time is short,
and, indeed, it seems to her shorter than it is. God so
fixes Himself in the interior of this soul, that when she

[1] Rather, " He who joins himself to the Lord is one with him in
spirit " (1 Co 6¹⁷). We do not need to accept Teresa's exegesis.
There is here no thought of a marriage union. " This is the same
unio mystica which Jesus Himself so often demands in the Gospel
of John, and in which no ethical diversity exists between the spirit
of the believing men and the spirit of Christ which fills it " (Meyer).

comes to herself she cannot but believe she was in God, and that God was in her. This truth is so deeply rooted in her that, though many years may pass away before God bestows the like favour upon her, she never forgets it. . . . But you will ask me how the soul saw it or understood it ? I answer, she did not see it then, but afterwards she sees it clearly ; and this is not so much a vision as a certitude which remains in the soul, and which God only can infuse into her. . . . But how can that have a certainty which we see not ? I do not know; it is His work : but I know that what I say is true, and whoever has not this certainty, I should say it was not a union of the soul with God, but of some faculty or some other of the many kinds of favour which God bestows on the soul." [1]

While, then, there can be no doubt concerning the fact of the mystics' ardent longing after union with God, or concerning their belief in the possibility of such union being effected, it cannot be said that they have succeeded in definitely determining either its essential nature or its precise degree. " In all these things," declares Teresa, " we must not seek to know the reasons for seeing how they are done, since our understanding cannot comprehend them." But does this also apply to the *manner* of attaining the desired, if indefinable, union with God ? Do we look in vain to the mystics for any definite statement on this point ? The calm and sane language of William Law should help us here. This is what he says : " God, the only Good of all intelligent natures, is not an absent or distant God, but is more present in and to our souls than our own bodies ; and we are strangers to heaven and without God in the world, for this only reason, because we are void of that spirit of prayer which alone can unite, and never fails to unite us with the One only Good, and to open heaven and the kingdom of God within us. . . . For the sun meets not the springing bud that stretches towards him with half that certainty as God, the source of all good, communicates Himself to the soul that longs to partake of Him." [2] In the judgement of this great mystic, therefore, there is one way, and only one way, by which the soul can reach union with God, and that is through the spirit of prayer.

[1] *The Interior Castle* (Fifth Abode).   [2] *The Spirit of Prayer*, p. 5.

PART V

MYSTICISM IN ENGLISH POETRY

WILLIAM WORDSWORTH AS LEADING REPRESENTATIVE

IN his concluding lecture on Nature-Mysticism, Dr.
Inge makes two interesting observations. One is
that in contrast to their predecessors the later Christian
mystics recognize that there is no incongruity between
the natural and the spiritual, the external world being
" the living vesture of the Deity " ; and the other, that
the poet is more alive to the Divine in Nature than either
the theologian or the naturalist.

By thus taking up a more appreciative attitude towards
the visible creation than that of William Law or the
Cambridge Platonists, the later mystics put forward a
new evaluation of the religious teaching of Nature. And
if, in so far as this found expression in poetry, it necessarily
took the form of meditative musing rather than that of
direct practical instruction, it served at least to bring
about a more intelligent appreciation of spiritual truth
by presenting it in the light of analogies from the natural
world. Moreover, as Inge reminds us, this was the method
employed by Jesus Himself as a Lover of Nature, by many
of the Greek Fathers, and in the Roman Church notably
by St. Francis of Assisi. But by the beginning of the
thirteenth century, or at least from Chaucer downwards,
there had set in a change. In Spenser's *Hymn of Heavenly
Beauty* " that sovereign light " which " kindles the love
of God " is still represented as causing " loathing of this
vile world," but this point of view, which had been widely
prevalent for two or three hundred years, had begun to
disappear. The love of nature is not absent from either
the humanists of the Renaissance or the German and
Swiss leaders of the Reformation, while the writings of St.
Francis de Sales and others shew that among French

mystics, too, the outer world was viewed as reflecting the goodness and beauty of its Maker. And surely they were right in repudiating the idea that to depreciate the handiwork of the Creator betokens spiritual-mindedness, and in hailing every advance in scientific knowledge as an enhancement of the glory and beauty of the material universe.[1]

Without entering upon the question of the poet's superiority to either the theologian or the naturalist in apprehending the Divine in the facts and appearances of nature, it may safely be said that of the type of mysticism which finds in communion with nature an interpretation of the higher realm of spiritual truth the leading representative is the poet Wordsworth. There were others, such as Crashaw (?1613–49), Henry Vaughan, "the Silurist" (1622–95), Coleridge (1772–1834), Tennyson (1809–92), and Browning (1812–89), but among them all in this respect William Wordsworth is supreme.

That all natural appearances, whether on a grander scale as in the lines :

> The sounding cataract
> Haunted me like a passion ; the tall rock,
> The mountain, and the deep and gloomy wood,
> Their colours and their forms, were then to me
> An appetite,

or, in a minuter aspect, as *e.g.* the fields and the flowers, the green corn, the bare trees, the brooks and fountains, the birds and the young lambs. attracted his keenest interest, is obvious to every reader. Indeed, he frankly calls himself " a worshipper of Nature." Through the analogies it furnishes, the symbolism of nature was to him the key to the mystery and the meaning of life. He sought no airy, whimsical flights, but strictly conformed to the test by which Dr. Inge so clearly distinguishes between real symbolism and its fanciful distortion when he

[1] It may not be inappropriate to note that when in *A Short Statement of the Church's Faith* commended by the General Assembly of the Church of Scotland (1935) it is expressly declared that " The Church welcomes the knowledge brought to light by scientific inquiry into all the facts of nature and history, in the assurance that all true understanding of these facts will serve to shew forth the glory of God," this is entirely in line with the attitude of the later Christian Mysticism.

says : " The symbolic value of all natural objects is not
that they remind us of something that they are not, but
that they help us to understand something that they in
part are."

By Nature, " his lifelong mistress," Wordsworth
usually means the external world as alive, or animated
by a soul. He conceives it as a personality imparting
to everything its distinctive life and work ; in short, as the
all-pervading Spirit of God. In this way the idea of God
is transferred to an actual person whom he creates, " to
a Being whom he terms Nature." [1] The life of Nature is
depicted as a life of joy and peace and brotherly fellowship based on the mutual love of every constituent part.
Viewed thus, Nature is Divine, because, living in its manifold forms, God is always giving and receiving Himself
throughout the world. Our communion, however, is
not with the imaginary creation, but with the Spirit of
God who is the life of all. Although Wordsworth discerns
in Nature features resembling those of the life in Man,
that is in *human* Nature, and describes Nature and Man as
essentially adapted to each other—" the external world
is fitted to the Mind "—he clearly differentiates between
them. His position is practically that expressed by
St. Paul : " The earnest expectation of the creature
waiteth for the manifestation of the sons of God." In the
life of Nature speaking to us through the things of sense,
and by her heaven-inspired teaching, we are taught of
God and united to Him. In order to this, however, Man
must possess the childlike heart of love which alone can
appreciate the beauty of the world. Nature will not appeal
to those who value

> the transcendent universe
> No more than as a mirror that reflects
> To proud self-love her own intelligence.

To apprehend Nature's teaching demands also a reverent,
worshipful spirit, purity of heart, and freedom from selfish
worldly mindedness.

> The world is too much with us ; late and soon,
> Getting and spending, we lay waste our powers :
> Little we see in Nature that is ours ;
> We have given our hearts away, a sordid boon.

---

[1] Stopford A. Brooke, *Theology in the English Poets*, Lec. VI.

From true sensibility to the influences of Nature, on the other hand, the soul advances to the love of God as Father, Redeemer, and Comforter.

After completing his studies at Cambridge, Wordsworth felt the overpowering influence of Nature upon him give way somewhat, but soon there set in a reaction in which, through her Divine voice heard in solitude, he recognized himself to be " a dedicated spirit." Touring in France and Switzerland shortly before the Revolution of 1793, he was keenly susceptible to the majestic sublimities of the Alps, and the awe and joy of soul thereby induced led him into union with the God of the universe. In France, again, he became an ardent republican ; and, being obliged to return from a second visit to that country by the stoppage of his allowances, left it probably just in time to escape falling a victim to the guillotine on account of his strong sympathy with the Girondists. By these experiences his interest both in Nature and in Man was stimulated, and the two fused as by an alchemy of the spirit into a marriage union. The beauty of Nature he represents as a revelation. Through Nature, God had revealed to him the worth and dignity of his soul, as well as the reverence due to scientific truth and elevated poetry.

Meanwhile, then, from love of Nature, combined as that was with a profound sense of the dignity of peasant life, there had been developed in our poet the love of Man. Man he conceived as the crown of Nature,

> As, of all visible creatures, crown, though born
> Of dust, and kindred to the worm ; a Being
> Both in perception and discernment, first
> In every capability of rapture,
> Through the divine effect of power and love ;
> As, more than anything we know, instinct
> With Godhead,

and " as reflected through him human nature seems an emanation from the Trinity." Especially was it the spirit of humanity in the aggregate, in universal Man, rather than in individual men, that impressed him. Without being blind to the sin and misery of the human race, he realized its retention of the Divine and its potentialities of good as " one Brotherhood held in one Father." The

teaching of the French Revolution, that Man is one and
indivisible, was welcomed by him as a believer in

> the government of equal rights
> And individual worth.

Even the tumultuous present, in which nothing was left
of liberty but the crimes perpetrated in her name, could
not, however, uproot either his faith in freedom or his
love for the romantic past, though it temporarily robbed
his poetry of its power. It was mainly his Christian belief
that rescued him from the gloom produced by " despair
of the present and regret of the past." In renouncing the
standpoint of the Revolution he had also to renounce at
least part of the Christian elements bound up with it.
The travesty of Christianity which had been set up was
only an emasculated caricature of its real character, and
wholly ignored its assertion of the equality of rights, its
consideration for the poor, and its emphasis on the duties
of men as exercisers of their rights. What was swept away
was only its ecclesiastical and political trappings ; what
was fundamental to Christianity remained, and in republicanism blossomed afresh. For republicanism was
really but the application of the principles of Christanity
to the relations of men as brothers, as members of the
commonwealth, as citizens of the world, and as children
of the one great Father. It was given to Wordsworth to
perceive this, and as there dawned upon his mind not
only the vision of a world in which no man should be in
bondage, but also that of a glorious future for the race,
he became inspired with a new song. Beyond any other
English poet he has woven into the texture of the principles
for which the Revolution stood the analogous truths of
the Christian faith. An enthusiastic love for Man—
especially for those of the common order, and for nations
oppressed by despotic tyranny—and an eager longing for
the overthrow of every form of wrong, had led to an
abandonment of the atheistic tendency to view all things
" in disconnexion dull and spiritless," and to a full restoration of his trust in God. It became clear to him that the
cause of Man was likewise the cause of God. If after the
welcome defeat of Napoleon at Waterloo his ardour cooled
somewhat, both in respect of his love of liberty and his

hatred of oppression, this must be attributed partly to an innate conservatism, and partly to the mellowing influence of advancing years. By the war against France, as well as by the Reign of Terror, the foundations of his love of Nature and of Man had indeed been rudely shaken. Further reflection, however, shewed him that Divine retributive and " everlasting Justice " had been at work in the tribulations of France, and that in view of the virtues which inspired the sufferings of self-sacrifice there was still a gleam of hope for Man.

As a whole, Wordsworth's poetry testifies that his was essentially " the philosophic mind." Though some of it is marked by extreme simplicity, almost degenerating into silliness, and though in the expression of his philosophical opinions he is often mystical and sometimes unintelligible, it is true to say that throughout it gives evidence of real intellectual power. The simple is not necessarily the shallow, nor is the abstruse essentially full of thought. Wordsworth, however, can probe the depths of speculative philosophy as well as sing in the simple strains of *Lucy Gray* or *We are Seven*. As will be more particularly noted in the sequel, distinct echoes of the Platonic philosophy are heard in his famous *Ode on Intimations of Immortality*, and *The Excursion*,[1] so much criticized on various grounds, and much of which indeed can scarcely be reckoned poetry, at all events makes it clear that he was conversant with problems concerning not only metaphysics and theology, but science, national education, economics, and politics as well. If its themes are somewhat prosaic, its theories and arguments are far from being so. Speaking of the English poets of the nineteenth century, Stopford Brooke calls him " greatest not only as a poet, but as a philosopher," and goes on to say : " It is the mingling of profound thought, and of ordered thought, with poetic sensibility and power (the power always the master of the sensibility), which places him in this high position. . . . The whole of his

[1] *The Excursion* forms only the second of three divisions of a projected poem to be entitled *The Recluse*. *The Prelude*, dealing autographically with the growth of a poet's mind, was not published till after Wordsworth's death. Part of Division I. of *The Recluse* was written, but Division III. was never even begun.

poetry is full, not of systematic theology, but of his own theology." [1]

Wordsworth's views regarding the nature of God are coloured by his Platonism. According to Dr. Inge his theology has its roots in a profound " sense of the boundless " :

> I have felt
> A presence that disturbs me with the joy
> Of elevated thoughts : a sense sublime
> Of something far more deeply interfused,
> Whose dwelling is the light of setting suns,
> And the round ocean, and the living air,
> And the blue sky, and in the mind of man
> A motion, and a spirit that impels
> All thinking things, all objects of all thoughts,
> And rolls through all things.

Not unfittingly, this has been called the " higher Pantheism," to distinguish it from the usual connotation of that term. The poet's conception is that of a Divine intelligence inherent in and pervading, while yet distinct from and transcending, all nature. But although, as one who had through nature reached contact with the Divine, he accepts the doctrine of immanence, he expressly states that " he does not look upon Nature and God as the same." If he holds that God reveals Himself in nature, he also affirms that He is Himself more than nature.

In so far as we can trace Wordsworth's spiritual development from its reflection in his poetry, its starting-point is to be found in his peculiarly contemplative spirit and his marked tendency towards solitary meditation. A modern Isaac, he " went out to meditate in the field." Referring in general terms to the themes, the scenes, and the joys of his contemplative thought, he says :

> On man, on nature, and on human life
> Musing in solitude, I oft perceive
> Fair strains of imagery before me rise,
> Accompanied by feelings of delight
> Pure, or with no unpleasing sadness mixed.

To begin with, he was more concerned with Nature than with Man. He avows that for a time nature was with

[1] *Op. cit.* Lec. V.

him " all in all," but in the same poem proceeds to register
a consciously higher attainment in spiritual life :

> For I have learned
> To look on nature, not as in the hour
> Of thoughtless youth, but hearing oftentimes
> The still, sad music of humanity.

Underlying much of Wordsworth's poetry is the Platonic
doctrine of pre-existence and reminiscence,[1] though in a
form coloured by Christianity.   The Greek philosopher's
belief was grounded on his conception of Ideas (*e.g.* truth,
justice, love, etc.) as real existences constituting Eternal
Being, beheld by and inspiring the heavenly deities.   This
vision is shared by every soul in its pre-mundane life, but
the vision is only in part, and transient at that.   In its
human and worldly state the soul is tripartite—rational,
sensual, and spiritual.   Its earthly existence is passed in
an endeavour to regain through recollection " the vision
splendid."   The sight of beauty recalls " the visionary
gleam," but in its attempted upward flight the spiritual
is impeded by the sensual soul, which is alive merely to
the earthly side of beauty.   There is thus, in Plato's
imagery, a contested race between a white steed and a
black, the one exemplifying the rational, and the other
the sensual, soul.   Only after a severe struggle can the
heavenly vision be recovered and life eternal won.   While
attracted by the ideas of pre-existence and reminiscence,
Wordsworth simply links on his own thought with them—
in what manner is shown in the following well-known
extracts from the *Ode* :

> Our birth is but a sleep and a forgetting :
> The soul that rises with us, our life's star,
> Hath elsewhere had its setting,
> And cometh from afar ;

---

[1] According to Plato's *Phædo*, all true knowledge consists in
reminiscence or recollection of Ideas familiar to it in a previous
state of existence.   His doctrine of immortality is based upon the
religious conviction that the soul of man is related to and partici-
pates in the Divine idea of life, with which it is almost co-ordinated.
In the *Philetus*, one of the later dialogues, when discoursing upon
Memory as the basis of desire, Plato is silent with regard to this
doctrine of recollection, and his silence is perhaps rightly interpreted as marking a stage in his mental growth.

Not in entire forgetfulness,
    And not in utter nakedness,
But trailing clouds of glory do we come,
        From God, who is our home :
    Heaven lies about us in our infancy !

Those shadowy recollections,
    Which be they what they may,
Are yet the fountain light of all our day,
Are yet a master light of all our seeing.

Hence in a season of calm weather,
        Though inland far we be,
Our souls have sight of that immortal sea
        Which brought us hither ;
    Can in a moment travel thither,—
And see the children sport upon the shore,
And hear the mighty waters rolling evermore.

In particular, Wordsworth parts company with Plato
when he portrays the child as nearer to God and the
beatific vision than the man. Whereas in this respect the
philosopher would give the palm to the sage, the English
poet declares that under earthly influences childhood's
impressions of " the glory and the brightness of the world "
begin to decay in youth, and in manhood " die away,"
the man being thus caused to lose sight of

            the glories he hath known
    And that imperial Palace whence he came.

With an observant eye on the changing phenomena of
nature, the details of which he invests with an atmosphere
of poetic sensibility, of a thoughtful and contemplative
mood of mind, and instinctively a Platonist, Wordsworth
writes also as one strongly influenced by Christian doctrine.
Apart altogether from his attitude towards ecclesiastical
organization, which became more favourable as he grew
older, there is scant reason to call in question the reality
of his Christian faith. Yet, although admittedly he shows
a truly reverent spirit, his standpoint has been stigmatized
as non-Christian. The criticism, however, simply amounts
to this, that he never writes in distinctly evangelical
language of the conventional order. If he found the real
substance of the Atonement in the Incarnation rather
than in the Crucifixion, is this a sufficient reason for refusing
him the name of Christian ? Then the Greek Fathers,

and many others, must share the same condemnation. And at the least, before acquiescing in the slur thus sought to be cast upon him, it is only just to weigh his own testimony. In a letter to his friend Sir George Beaumont, dated May 28, 1825, Wordsworth writes : " I look abroad upon Nature, I think of the best part of our species, I lean upon my friends, and I meditate upon the Scriptures, especially the Gospel of St. John, and my creed rises up of itself, with the ease of an exhalation, yet a fabric of adamant." This is in effect a confession of faith, and indicates that his Christianity is beyond question. Again, writing to Dean Alford on February 21, 1840, he expressly gives his reasons for refraining from the insertion of definitely Christian matter into even his later poems. For one thing, he was deterred from doing so by an instinctive reticence with regard to sacred things, and, for another, by his desire to avoid inadvertently falling into error in giving poetical expression to matters of doctrine. " I have," he says, " been averse to frequent mention of the mysteries of Christian faith ; not from a want of a due sense of their momentous nature, but the contrary. I felt it far too deeply to venture on handling the subject as familiarly as many scruple not to do. I am far from blaming them, but let them not blame me. I might err in points of faith, and I should not deem my mistakes less to be deprecated because they were expressed in metre." Evidently he considered that there are subjects too high for poetry, or, as St. Paul says, " words not lawful to utter "—the secret ecstatic possession of the mystical soul. In some directions he frankly deviated from the orthodox creed. For instance, so far from shewing any appreciation of the confessional doctrine of original sin, he speaks of his infant daughter's " sinless progress " through a world of care, and portrays her as like the moon " free from stain." His theology may, of course, be quite fairly criticized, but his Christian faith in general is surely beyond dispute. A touching picture of his deeply devotional spirit is presented as in his old age he writes :

> I bent before Thy gracious throne,
>   And asked for peace on suppliant knee,
> And peace was given—nor peace alone,
>   But faith sublimed to ecstasy.

What was characteristic of Wordsworth's poetry in its mystical aspect may be briefly summed up as consisting of : (1) The striking freshness and subtlety of his view of nature. For him it is a mystic text calling for exposition and explanation. " The maxims of Wordsworth's form of natural religion were uttered before Wordsworth only in the sense in which the maxims of Christianity were uttered before Christ." [1] (2) The claim that " the child is father of the man," and that through childhood's recollection of a previous and apparently sinless existence in a higher state, stimulated for a time by external nature, we are furnished with " some shadows of eternity," and with a basis for philosophical study. As a Christian mystic he clearly exhibits both of these features when he makes bold to say :

> Happy those early days when I
> Shined in my angel infancy !
> Before I understood this place
> Appointed for my second race,
> Or taught my soul to fancy aught
> But a white, celestial thought ;
> When yet I had not walked above
> A mile or two from my first Love,
> And looking back at that short space
> Could see a glimpse of His bright face ;
> When on some gilded cloud or flower
> My gazing soul would dwell an hour,
> And in those weaker glories spy
> Some shadows of eternity ;
> Before I taught my tongue to wound
> My conscience with a sinful sound,
> Or had the black art to dispense
> A several sin to every sense,
> But felt through all His fleshly dress
> Bright shoots of everlastingness.

---

[1] F. W. H. Myers, in *English Men of Letters*, p. 130.

INDEX

Francis de Sales, St., 60 f., 65 ff., 73, 90.
Franciscans, 26.
Frank, Sebastian, 37, 95.
Free Spirit, Brethren of the, 21 f., 31 f., 85, 126.
Friars of the Mitigation, 55.
" Friends of God," 29, 36.
Froude, 46.
Funken (="Spark") in Eckhart, 28, 40, 87.

Galen, 36.
Gass, 16.
Gerson, John Charlier de, 32 f.
Gibbon, 113, 120 f.
Gieseler, 129.
Glanvil, 109.
Graham, Mrs. Cunninghame, 45.
Granger, Geneviève, 74.
Greek Fathers, the, 41, 140.
Gregory, E. C., 52.
Gröndal, community of, 32.
Groot, Gerard, 32.
Guyon, Madame, 62, 72 ff.

Hafiz, Persian poet, 17.
Harnack, A., 2, 11, 15, 86 ff.
Herman, E., 1, 41, 126 f.
Herrmann, W., 89 f.
Hilton, Walter, 40 f.
Hobbes, 104.
Hügel, Baron von, 126 f.
Hus, John, 33, 36.

Imitation of Christ, The, 33 f., 39.
Inge, W. R., 11, 25, 30, 39 ff., 90, 100, 111.
Inquisition, the, 5, 29, 42, 55, 61 f., 76.
Islam, 16 f.
Issy, Articles of, 79.

Jamblichus, 13.
James, William, 3 f., 17, 99.
Jeanne de Chantal, 55 ff.
Jesuits, the, 60 ff.
Jesus, the historic, 9, 37, 39, 48, 63.
Joachim of Floris, 21, 29.
Johannine Mysticism, 6 ff.
Juliana of Norwich, 39 f.

Kabbala, the, 5, 37.
Kelly, J. Fitzmaurice, 46.
Kempis, Thomas à, 32 ff., 39, 73, 88.
Kingsley, Charles, 15.
Koràn, 16.
Koràn worship, 5.
Kurz, 98.

La Combe, Father, 74 f., 77.
La Mothe, Father, 75 ff.
Lange, J. P., 5.
Law, William, 87, 90, 98, 111 ff., 127 f., 131 ff.
Lewis, David, 54.
Locke's *Essay*, 111.
Logos, the, in Philo, 11; in St. John, 6, 14; in Plutarch, 11; in Plotinus' Nous=Logos of St. John, 14.
Luther, Martin, 34 ff., 38 f., 44.

Maintenon, Madame de, 77 f.
Martensen, 98.
Maurice, F. D., 98.
Maximus the Confessor, 16, 20.
Mechtildis of Magdeburg, 29.
Melanchthon, 30, 44.
Meyer, 130.
Milton, 125.
Molinos, 59 ff, 76; special points in his teaching, 62 ff.
More, Henry, 98, 109 f.
Münster, Anabaptist movement in, 36.
Münster, Thomas, 39.
Myers, F. W. H., 142.
Mysticism, meaning of, 1–4; in the Scriptures, 5 ff.; in Johannine writings, 6 ff.; in Pauline epistles, 8 f.; in Persian poetry, 17; partly reconciled with Scholasticism, 24; relation of, to the Reformation, 38 f.; in England in pre-Reformation times, 39 ff.; basic principles and main features of Christian Mysticism, 123 ff.
Mystics, rationalistic and pantheistic, 21; ascetic, 22, 39.

PRINTED BY
MORRISON AND GIBB LTD.
EDINBURGH AND LONDON

Q